The Art

Design Your Mind to Destroy Limitations, Unleash Your Inner-Greatness, and Achieve the Success of Your Dreams

Stellan Moreira

About the Author

Stellan Moreira is young and motivated entrepreneur and best-selling author on a mission to change himself, and the world.

While he may be young, his information is valuable. He is self-educated, and he plans on instilling a certain sense of understanding within each reader that he has been fortunate to be able to instill within himself. This understanding has allowed him to accomplish so much, and keeps him constantly looking forward with gratitude, understanding, and determination to reach all his goals. Not only this, but it has allowed him to truly understand himself, and find a beautiful sense of peace and happiness he has always longed for. From this point onward, he realized that we wanted and needed to share his values, thoughts, information, and beliefs with the rest of the world. He realized that each individual has a meaningful purpose, and he put it upon himself to place great effort towards helping as many people find and realize their own.

His sincere mission and purpose is to help as much as he possibly can. He wants you to do the best in everything, and he wants you to succeed. What most people don't realize is that they already possess all the powers needed to make their lives completely filled with happiness, peace, wealth, and abundance, and the only thing truly standing in their way is themselves: the limiting thoughts and beliefs that they harbor in their minds. These beliefs tell them that they can't accomplish their dreams, that they can't be happy, and that they can't live the life they wish they were meant for. He is here to tell you right now that these thoughts are beyond untrue. They are so false, and yet we constantly allow them to successfully blind each and every one of us from our true potential.

Stellan is here to completely change this. He is here to make a difference in each and every readers lives.

He will never stop, for this is only the beginning.

The power of the mind is limitless; utilize it, and live a life beyond worth living.

-   **Stellan Moreira**

This book is dedicated to family: we love you, and appreciate everything you have done for us. For without you, we would be nothing.

I love you bayboo: forever and always.

Thank you.

Follow **StellanMoreira** for book updates & free offers, inspiring content, motivational stories, and other resources to help you wire your "growth" mentality, achieve profound success, and *"live a life beyond worth living."*

 **StellanMoreira**

 **StellanMoreira**

 **StellanMoreira**

The Art of Belief

By

Stellan Moreira

In no way is it legal to reproduce, duplicate, or transmit any part of this document in either electronic means or in printed format. Recording of this publication is strictly prohibited and any storage of this document is not allowed unless with written permission from the publisher. All rights reserved.

The information provided herein is stated to be truthful and consistent, in that any liability, in terms of inattention or otherwise, by any usage or abuse of any policies, processes, or directions contained within is the solitary and utter responsibility of the recipient reader. Under no circumstances will any legal responsibility or blame be held against the publisher for any reparation, damages, or monetary loss due to the information herein, either directly or indirectly.

Respective authors own all copyrights not held by the publisher.

The information herein is offered for informational purposes solely, and is universal as so. The presentation of the information is without contract or any type of guarantee assurance.

The trademarks that are used are without any consent, and the publication of the trademark is without permission or backing by the trademark owner. All trademarks and brands within this book are for clarifying purposes only and are the owned by the owners themselves, not affiliated with this document.

Table of Contents

Introduction

Thank you for taking the time to read this. This book is filled with the proper information, motivation, and guidance that will not only allow you, but push you towards completely changing your life for the better. Not only this, but this book will aid you in realizing your full, unlimited potential, which will allow you to unleash your **inner-greatness**, and **create the life of your dreams.**

But first, you must fully implement what it teaches into every aspect of your life.

P.S. Pay attention to the **bold.**

"Your beliefs become your thoughts, your thoughts become your words, your words become your actions, your actions become your habits, your habits become your values, and your values become your destiny." – **Mahatma Gandhi**

Do you ever wonder why you are living the kind of life you are currently living? Do you ever consider why it might be that your life feels somewhat unfulfilled, while it seems like others are living full, meaningful, and purposeful lives?

While you could have many explanations and justifications as to why you have not attained much in life, the truth lies in your beliefs. **_You are whoever you are and you are living a certain kind of life solely because of the beliefs you nurture._** Nurture the right, healthy, positive beliefs and you will enjoy an abundant, happy, and successful life. Nurture the wrong beliefs - ones that make you feel unconfident, limited, and unhappy - and you will manifest nothing but sorrow, and an unfulfilled life.

Where are your beliefs derived from? What exactly is the essence of your beliefs? Like Gandhi described it, your life solely depends on the kind of beliefs you nurture and, along with this, your **beliefs** are completely dependent on the **thoughts** you sustain in your mind.

As a famous old proverb states, **"As a man thinketh, so is he."**

This proverb contains a powerful hidden truth. It portrays that you have the ultimate power of turning your life around, transforming it for the better, and living the life you are truly meant for: the life of your **dreams**. Yes, you: You are the sole owner of your life and you have full authority over it. While you may think that things are destined to be a certain way and you can never fully control all aspects of your life, the truth is the complete **opposite: you are the ultimate creator of your own reality.**

You have a beautiful, amazing, and extraordinary mind; this is the same for everyone. All of us have the capability to think, and the thoughts we nurture and support shape the **entire course of our life**.

Do you ever wonder why accomplished people like Tony Robbins, Jim Carrey, Steve Jobs, and Warren Buffet achieved incredible amount of fame, wealth, and abundance, despite having experienced extreme poverty, hardships, and obstacles? While you may think it was because the universe was kinder to them, this is once again not true. The truth is that all these people achieved everything they dreamt of because of the positive and unlimited thoughts they harbored and nurtured in their minds. They told themselves that they could create something truly beautiful and significant, **so they did**. They told themselves that they can accomplish anything they placed their mind and heart on, **so they did**. They told themselves that they are **unlimited in every single way possible,** so they took the leap forward, and began creating their destiny from scratch.

This goes for anyone that has ever achieved profound success in absolutely anything; if you have ever found yourself envying a friend who started small and was not as stable as you were at a time, but is now living a wonderful and fulfilled life, this is also because of the sort of beliefs that friend supported.

Suppose your friend is a "he".

Your friend believed in himself. Your friend nurtured his mind with a constant supply of positive thoughts that, overtime, turned into strong, healthy beliefs that completely changed and improved his life for the better. Your friend chose to believe in the things he wanted to manifest in his life, and that is exactly what he did. As Karen Marie Moning said, *"what you choose to believe makes you the person you are."*

If you are not proud of yourself and the kind of life you have built so far, lay the blame on your thoughts and beliefs. Fortunately, however, by changing your thoughts and beliefs, you can change the entire course of your life. You can make your life brighter, better, more beautiful, and more meaningful than it has ever been before: all you must do is **believe**.

If you want abundance, you **can** accomplish that. If you want heaps of wealth, you **can** actualize that. Happiness, good health, spirituality, love, healthy relationships, an attractive physique, and all the riches in life: all these things can be yours, but **only** if you nurture the right thoughts, and transform them into powerful beliefs you will live by for the rest of your life.

If, and only if, you feed yourself with powerful, progressive, and positive thoughts, and then believe in them with all your **heart** and **mind**, can you manifest all of your desires. Your beliefs are your ideologies: the concepts and viewpoints you vehemently believe in that direct and run your life. Beliefs emanate from the incessant trickle of little to big thoughts that run in your mind and deposit their many neutral, positive, and negative impressions upon you.

Your mind can be compared to a gigantic cave composed of many dissimilar caverns. Each cavern hosts a series of similar thoughts that, when strengthened by constantly pondering on them or thinking in a similar direction, form a set of beliefs. Over time, some of those beliefs have grown amazingly strong and indestructible and are now sort of set in stone whereas others are brittle, thin, and easy to break. While you can easily take over the brittle beliefs, with consistent effort, you can also break the apparently hard ones.

Your thoughts are the essence and building blocks of your beliefs; if you change them, you can modify and improve your beliefs as well. We are indeed creatures of thought. By controlling our thoughts, we can alter our beliefs and then bring any necessary adjustments into our life.

How can we do that? What sort of effort do we need to exert to create beliefs that can cast their wonderful magic on our life and make it as sparkling as we want?

Well, that is the purpose of this book.

'The Art of Belief' shall help you fully comprehend the power and significance your beliefs have over your life. It shall then proceed to teach you, in a systematic manner, how to nurture amazing beliefs. Get started with this blueprint so you can unleash your inner-power that to this date, you were unaware of.

Thank you again for choosing to read this book. I strongly believe that it will inspire and prompt you to take massive action to change the course of your life.

Along with nurturing our thoughts and beliefs, we must also create powerful habits that will lead us toward achieving profound success in everything we do. In order to help you realize the correct habits you must maintain to create a fulfilled, significant life, I have created my own self-comprised list of 27 powerful habits that, if implemented, will wire your mind for success, allow you to become truly happy, and push you toward achieving the greatest amount of financial freedom. I have placed this list in my previous book, "Million Dollar Habits". I strongly advise that you read both "Million Dollar Habits," and "The Art of Belief," for these two books go hand-in-hand in teaching one how to create a truly beautiful life filled with nothing other than health, wealth, and happiness.

Click here to get your copy of "Million Dollar Habits"

Part 1

The Creation of Belief and the Belief of Creation

"Man often becomes what he believes himself to be. If I keep on saying to myself that I cannot do a certain thing, it is possible that I will end by really becoming incapable of doing it. On the contrary, if I shall have the belief that I can do it, I shall surely acquire the capacity to do it even if I may not have it at the beginning." – **Mahatma Gandhi**

Gandhi was right on point; if you keep feeding yourself a certain suggestion repeatedly, you start to believe it and once you believe something so strongly, it becomes a part of your reality.

How do we create beliefs and what are the things we should believe in to manifest a beautiful life? In the first chapter of the book, we shall reveal this and much more. The chapters of part 1 of this book aim to help you truly understand two concepts: **The**

Creation of Belief, and **The Belief of Creation.**

In other words: creating the most sincere and powerful beliefs within yourself, so that you could manifest your own personalized, powerful, and fulfilling life.

Chapter 1

The Creation of Belief

'Faith is expectancy. You do not receive what you want, you do not receive what you pray for, not even what you say you have faith in; you will always receive what you actually expect." – **Eric Butterworth**

Eric Butterworth is indeed right: you constantly manifest things you truly expect to happen. If you expect something terrible to happen to you and you keep believing that pesky, little voice inside you, something terrible will indeed happen to you. To manifest an amazing life, you must first believe in the right things.

What should you believe in and how do we create beliefs? Let us find out.

Seeing is not always Believing

"Seeing is not believing; believing is seeing! You see things, not as they are, but as you are." – **Eric Butterworth**

While many people think 'seeing is believing', this notion is completely false. In truth, how could you ever expect to see something if you never truly believe you'll see it in the first place? Although this may be correct for many things, it certainly isn't for creating your own successful and fulfilling life. The fact is, in order to actually **see** something within your life, you must first truly **believe** that you will. If you want to see more money in your bank account, you must sincerely believe that this is a possibility, and then act on it and begin finding ways to attain more money. Martin Luther King Jr. once said, "Seeing is not always believing." This implies that to nurture a belief, you need not see everything, but in order to see something, you must first powerfully believe that you will. Beliefs do not just come from seeing things around you; they are elements that take birth inside your mind.

A belief is an idea, concept, or notion you strictly adhere to and have faith in. As you can imagine, not all beliefs are strong; some of them are weak and easy to break. How strong or fragile a belief is depends solely on it

sincerity: the strength of your thoughts pertinent to that belief. If you strongly believe and have constant sincere thoughts that you will be successful and are going to attain everything you set your eyes on, you will ultimately attract great opportunities towards you that will help you manifest your dream.

How can you strongly believe in something? Are there certain criteria you need to fulfill?

To have a strong belief in something, you must keep in mind certain things.

1: Belief Comes Straight from Your Heart

Believing in something with all your might is indeed fundamental to **manifestation**: physically implementing a certain wish or desire within your reality. A belief is something so strong that even western rationalism and terrestrial logic fail to explain it. This is because a belief is completely relative, and it is something that is derived straight from the individuals inner-most self.

To have a strong belief in something, you must believe in it passionately from your soul. If you wish to be happy, feel yourself truly believe it. Do not question yourself and ask "Am I happy?" Instead, proclaim to yourself the following: "I am beyond happy. I am a genuine, amazing, and powerful person, and although I am not content with the current state of my life, I am truly happy because I know **I have the power to change it**." You must place the belief within yourself so profoundly that you will adhere to it as nothing other than **pure truth**. Only when you put your heart and soul into that belief shall you nurture progressive thoughts and take positive action that will push you towards completely altering that specific part of your life.

For instance, to become a wealthy and successful singer, you must believe in this goal with your all your mind, heart, and body. You must feel, from within you, that you can indeed become a famous, successful, and amazing singer loved by millions of fans across the world. If you believe in this goal with everything you have, you will force your mind and body to create thoughts and perform actions that will guide amazing experiences and opportunities towards you, and place you one step closer to actualizing your dreams.

Your heart holds unimaginable power. It is not just an organ made of flesh and veins; it has great authority, amazing abilities, and the potential to move mountains. That's not all: it is the center of our emotions; if you engage the heart in creating beliefs (by connecting these beliefs to the necessary emotions to propel you to action), you sleep, wake up, walk, and talk about your beliefs. In truth, this is the first step towards becoming successful. To unlock that power, you must simply believe in the ability of your heart to propel you in the direction you want to go. When you believe something is going to be true, your heart becomes invested in it emotionally and when your heart becomes fully engaged in a concept or notion, it signals your brain to create many similar thoughts (thoughts centered around taking action, and finding solutions). Even the Bible, in Matthew 6:21, aptly states; *"wherever your treasure is, there the desires of your heart will also be"*. The things you believe in are your treasures. If you have a strong belief about something, you will be emotionally connected to it in every way: you will love the process, no matter its duration, and you will love the outcomes – no matter what they may be.

For instance, see that your goal is to become more confident.

If you believe you are confident and your heart has produced the necessary emotional feelings associated with you becoming so, your brain will produce thoughts that will state you are confident, and, in turn, **you will be confident**.

If you keep believing you are self-assured and have complete faith in your capabilities, your brain will fire scores of such thoughts that will shape your feelings, attitudes, and behaviors in a similar manner. When many of your thoughts focus on one particular goal, they force you to start sincerely believing in it, making you behave accordingly. Thus, you begin to **feel confident**, **think confident**, and **act confident.**

Not only that, but these magical thoughts travel outside to the universe, interact with many similar thoughts, and attract towards you positive experiences that make you feel and become more confident.

As you can see, it all starts with getting your heart completely involved in a belief so it engages your mind in it too. Your job of manifesting something does not end here: you must also believe you have already achieved your desire.

2: Believe that You Have Achieved What You Want in the Present

The secret to manifesting a belief is to take that thing for granted. Do not get this wrong; it does not mean you should stop believing in it and stop strengthening your faith. Taking a belief for granted means you should believe you have already achieved that goal and you are enjoying it in the present. You take for granted only the things you have already achieved and those you are certain of.

For instance, if your desire is to become truly happy, tell yourself you already are, and believe it with your entire heart. Tell yourself, "Although I am not fully content with my life, I am happy. I am 100% happy, and now all I must do is work on improving the aspects of my life I am not content with." Feel your happiness travel all throughout your inner-self, throw a huge grin on your face, and smile towards the world. If you do this, I can guarantee the world will smile back.

Similarly, to utilize your beliefs as tools for manifesting something into your life, you must believe that the universe has already granted you your desire. The word 'grant' comes from the word 'credentem', which is of Latin origin and means 'to trust' or 'to believe.'

When you fully believe in something, you know that the universe will eventually grant you that wish (only with applied action, of course). This faith is what you need to make your beliefs come true. Whenever you set your eyes on a goal, be it a good job, a successful business, marrying the love of your life or having a baby, just believe you already have it in the present moment. Take it for granted and see how quickly you will turn that belief into your reality.

3: Believe in Something Passionately

This adds to the first point above. In addition to believing you have achieved what you want, you must be enamored of all that you wish to manifest. You must be completely and utterly in love with the idea or goal you want to create, and you must be 100% involved in it: love the process, understand and learn from your obstacles and adversities, and enjoy the outcomes. Great involvement comes from great passion and therefore, to be completely invested in an idea, you must have a powerful passion for it as well.

You cannot manifest something just to satisfy your mere curiosity or to prove something to others or yourself. You can only manifest something if you truly love it, and support it with a constant stream of genuine and positive thoughts and beliefs. If you follow the route of insincerity, you will not be fully involved in the process of your goal, you will not genuinely believe in it with all your heart, and, therefore, **you will not manifest it into your reality**.

To believe in something so strongly that it becomes your reality and a part of your destiny, you must attain a true, profoundly genuine and deep connection with it. You must truly want and yearn for that thing. You must crave it so much that you cannot live without it. When you want something so bad, you become as restless as a fish out of water: forcing you to do everything in your power to make that wish come true.

For that to happen, you need to be sincerely devoted to yourself and the universe surrounding you. You need to be honest to yourself about what you want, and then go out and get it. For instance, if you want wealth and abundance, be clear on the kind of wealth and abundance you want. Do you want to be a millionaire, or do you want just enough to supply yourself and your life with the things you need? Do you want money in abundance or is your search genuinely based on happiness in abundance? Be 100% clear about what you want so you can believe in it with sincerity and passion, and take action.

Your **'WHY'** for doing something must come from a place of complete understanding, truth, sincerity and passion.

- When you have full comprehension of something and understand every aspect of it, you know it inside out; this increases your involvement. For instance, if you have a clear understanding of the kind of love you want and the sort of soulmate you are looking for, you will become more involved in the idea of manifesting and searching for the love of your life, and achieving it in the most genuine way possible.

- When you believe something as the truth, you become sincere with it, which in turn drives your passion. For instance, if you believe you are a billionaire, you understand this goal to be true and a part of your being's destiny, which strengthens your sincerity and helps you manifest it.

- When you are passionate about something, every inch of your body yearns for it. When you have a massive desire for something, you are ready to put in as much hard work as required, and the harder and smarter you work for something, the quicker you manifest it. For instance, if you want to earn $10,000 a month and nothing you want exceeds your desire for this goal, you will work crazy for it. You will be ready to burn the midnight oil and will do everything in your power to make it true.

4: Make that Belief a Part of You

To manifest something, another criterion you need to fulfill is to make that corresponding belief a **constant** in your life. If you believe in something and you want to create that reality, you must make that belief a part of your existence.

When something becomes a part of your existence, naturally, you will believe in it, subconsciously think of it all the time, and act as if you have already manifested it in your present life. When something becomes a part of your subconscious, you begin to believe that you have attained it and like stated before, when you strongly believe the universe has granted you something, you begin to act and eventually achieve it.

This kind of belief comes from being indifferent to the belief you want to manifest. When you know you have already accomplished something, your state of indifference underpins that particular belief. This does not imply that you do not care about that thing. Instead, you become carefree about it because you know you have what you want.

When you attain something in your mental realm, your thoughts focus on it and your body works toward making it true in your physical reality. To make something true, that belief must become a sincere and genuine part of your being.

Having understood the criteria you need to fulfill to believe in something so strongly that you manifest it, let us see what you must do every day to create unwavering beliefs.

How to Create Unwavering Beliefs

- To create unwavering beliefs that help you manifest everything you want, first put your heart and soul in that belief.

- To make your heart want what you believe in, you must be clear and determined. Find out what you really want to manifest, and then become complete clear about it. Understand your goal so precisely that you have no ambiguity towards it. If you want good health, write down the state of health you desire; if you want to be spiritual, be clear on the kind of spirituality you aspire to achieve.

- Moreover, feel connected to that belief by becoming passionate about it. You must sincerely yearn for it, and be enthusiastic about achieving it; this is the only genuine way to accomplish anything. If you want to be a successful makeup artist, ask yourself if you genuinely want to achieve this goal.

- Believe you have achieved the thing you crave. Repeatedly tell yourself things like "I am successful," "I am happy," "I am wealthy," and other similar suggestions; this is the way to achieving success, happiness, and wealth. This process slowly imbeds that suggestion into your mind and when this happens, it becomes a part of you and you begin to become indifferent towards it. This means you accept and acknowledge you have actualized your desire, which in turn helps you make that belief come true.

Follow these guidelines and see how quickly you will create unwavering beliefs that establish and manifest all that you desire. In addition, you must also understand that you and your abilities are not limited; they do not have a cap: **even the sky is not the limit for those who do not see it as such**.

Chapter 2

The Belief of Creation: You Are Limitless

"If you are distressed by anything external, the pain is not due to the thing itself but to your own estimate of it; and this you have the power to revoke at any moment." –
Marcus Aurelius

If you pay close attention to the quote above, you will understand that you possess unlimited and unimaginable power. Your power roots in your beliefs and the power of belief is not limited at all: it is **infinite** and **boundless**. Only a limitless power can make you believe you are perfectly fine when a dangerous disease ravages you. Only an unrestricted power can make you feel you can achieve anything you want: even if everyone around you keeps saying you cannot.

Accomplishment Comes from Being Limitless

Great accomplishments always find root in great beliefs and great beliefs find root in a 'limitless' mindset. The only ones who achieve their desires are the ones who are willing to believe that extraordinary things can happen, those who believe in their goals, take full responsibility for the choices they make, and then actively pursue their dreams.

Every extraordinary, brilliant, and accomplished person who has ever been or is now on this earth followed this mantra, and through use of this mantra, manifested dreams came about. Take Bill Gate's example for instance. Had he believed that creating Microsoft was not possible, he would never have done so.

He was limitless; his mind was free from the confines of the rules set out by society, and he did not stop believing in himself or start believing his dream was a nearly impossible one. Instead, he went the extra mile and proved his worth thanks to his limitless beliefs.

Not only that, Gates suffered a great loss when his first business 'Traff-O-Data' failed miserably. That failure could have stopped him from believing in himself; he could have let it dampen his spirits, but he did not. Instead, he perceived it as an opportunity to become better and learn from his mistakes; he ended up accomplishing what nobody could ever dream of, and eventually reached the level of success he **believed** he was destined for.

Mother Teresa is another accomplished woman who portrayed the true power of a limitless mindset. She did not believe she could not show selfless care to hundreds of homeless children. She never believed it would be impossible for her to be so altruistic. Instead, she believed otherwise. She was so passionate about caring for others that she believed she could do anything she wanted for humanity; she proved herself right.

Another great example of supporting an infinite mindset is that of Richard Branson. He suffered dyslexia and his teachers at school were positive he would never make it big in the world. Richard, however, had other plans for himself. He stayed true to his beliefs, kept taking risks, and always had faith in his capabilities, which is how he ended up founding 'Virgin Records.'

These are only three examples of people who did not give in to societal pressures and instead believed in themselves, and kept pursuing their dreams. There are many others such as Michael Jordan, Stephen King, Steve Jobs, Thomas Edison, and Nelson Mandela. All these accomplished and well-known people lived a tough life. Most of them faced situations that obstructed their goals, or they did not have all the elements required to objectify their desires. Nonetheless, they eventually became successful and manifested what they wanted: solely because they knew they were **limitless**.

All these people surpassed the limitations thrown their way in the form of different obstacles. Instead of perceiving them as limitations, they observed them as growth opportunities: chances to help them become better and polish their skills. To be extraordinary, you must believe in your limitless power, and have faith in yourself constantly.

Let us see how you can do that.

The Power of the Universal Mind

A limitation is only a limitation if you believe and perceive it to be one. If your coach failed to select you for a swimming competition, and, in turn, you begin to believe you can never become a great swimmer, you will **never** become one. However, if you stop feeling restrained by that one setback and instead recommit to keep trying and moving forward, you will one day fulfill your dream.

Perception is indeed reality, and in order to create something (happiness, love, success), you must perceive it to be that way. If you do not perceive a limitation as a limitation, it will stop obstructing your own path. When nothing can keep you from moving forward, you will become **unstoppable**.

To become truly limitless, you must understand the true power of the Universal Mind: One, amazing and wise consciousness that suffuses our entire universe. Along with this, you must genuinely understand that you are a part of this Universal Mind. The

Universal Mind is extremely powerful, incredibly creative, knows everything, and is always present. This power takes full responsibility for the existence of possibility, and for helping most, if not all accomplished people actualize their dreams and goals.

To become limitless, you must first understand that your mind is a component of, and belongs to the Universal Mind. In order to do this, you must genuinely believe in your unlimited capabilities: **you have the power to do anything, learn anything, and become anyone**. Only when you believe your mind can harness the limitless potential of the Universal Mind shall you actually start utilizing it and manifesting all of your desires.

Einstein once said, *"Everything is energy and everyone is a part of the universe."* This portrays that all of us are of energy, and our existence is courtesy of the universal power around us. If we unite our mind with the Universal Mind, we can indeed become limitless, and achieve anything and everything we set out for ourselves.

The Universal Mind has some key characteristics that set it apart from everything else:

- The Universal Mind is 'All Knowing' aka **Omniscience**. By believing you are part of this one, Universal Mind, you are placing 100% faith in your capabilities. You are telling yourself that you can do, learn, and be absolutely anything you set your mind on, which will allow you to **destroy limitations, unleash your inner-greatness, and create the life of your dreams**. In this sense, when you see yourself as a part of the 'All Knowing' Universal Mind, you too will become 'All Knowing'.

- The Universal Mind is also **'Omnipotence'** meaning it is incredibly powerful and has the power to do anything and everything. By integrating your mind with the Universal Mind, you are classifying yourself as an energized, spiritual, and powerful being: one that has the capabilities to change oneself, and the entire surrounding world. Understanding

45

the truth behind your unlimited capabilities is the first step in fully comprehending and becoming one with the Universal Mind.

- The Universal Mind is also **'Omnipresent'** meaning it is present everywhere all the time. When you assimilate your mind with the Universal Mind, your power becomes omnipresent as well. No matter where you are, what you're doing, or who you're with, you will shed your light of limitless power and act on the belief that you are unlimited – attracting great opportunities and experiences towards you at all times.

By connecting your mind to the Universal Mind, you can tap into and use all of its abilities. You can attain full, unhindered access to its powers, its knowledge, its wisdom, its creativity, and its ability to turn the impossible into possible. When you can do that, **you can do anything**.

The words inscribed on the 'Ancient Greek Temple of Apollo' located at Delphi state,

"Know thyself and thou shalt know all the mysteries of the gods and the universe". This inscription indeed says it all: the power lies within you and your amazing mind. You can harness the power of the universe only by believing in yourself and by knowing your hidden realities. When you discover who you are and are aware of everything you want and need, you can better align yourself with the Universal Mind and make it a constant part of your life.

To stop living a life of limits, you must first **believe** in the Universal Mind. You must believe in its energy and its power. You must believe that the Universal Mind flows through you and everyone else in the universe and that the energy connects you to every being. This is how every being in the universe is interconnected and exactly how we become one with the Universal Mind. We also call this the 'Law of One' and the moment you start **believing** in this law, your mind will integrate with the Universal Mind, and become fully unstoppable.

Once you begin instilling your complete faith in the Universal Mind, you will start feeling its presence inside you. Since your mind is a composition of scores of thoughts, when you think you have unimaginable power, you start to nurture similar thoughts. The more you think in that direction, the more positive thoughts saturate your mind and when the right sort of thoughts enrich your mind, their energy and power becomes inconceivable.

By simply connecting yourself to the Universal Mind, you can harness the energy and power of everything and everyone around you. When you know nothing is separate from you and that everything is interconnected, you begin to experience everything you desire: happiness, good health, wealth, abundance, and true love. You must align yourself with the vibrational harmony of the universe and channelize that power; when you do this, the world shall be yours.

Now that you are aware of the limitless power in your possession as well as how, through the power of belief, you can become invincible, let us move on to discussing how you can consciously create your beliefs.

Chapter 3

Conscious Creation

"A life lived of choice is a life of conscious action. A life lived of chance is a life of unconscious creation." – **Neale Donald Walsch**

If you do not want to blame the universe for throwing meaningless and unwanted things your way, if you do not want to be someone who constantly complains of being unhappy and unsuccessful, and if you do not want to settle for mediocre things, you have to live a life of choice: *a life of consciously taken action*. This is indeed possible because you have the power to create your own reality. However, most people are not aware of this.

You may be unaware of the power of your thoughts, which is why you do not consciously create the life you want for yourself.

Let us dive deeper into this concept.

You are the Creator of Your Reality

We are all creators of our realities and our lives. Whether we are or are not happy with what we have created, this truth is one we cannot deny. A major reason why many of us cannot successfully manifest what we desire is our unawareness of our power: we are not aware that we hold the power to build and transform our lives, which is why we keep settling for whatever life throws our way instead of striving for better, amazing things. We are unconsciously creating things, which is why we do not always achieve our aspirations.

To opt for a better life, you must become conscious of this power. To create a life you would be happy to live, you must be more aware of your abilities, and the inner powers gifted to you. When you become more aware of your power and consciously utilize it as a tool to create the reality of your dreams, you practice 'conscious creation,' which allows you to personalize and transform any aspect of your life.

The conscious ability to create anything you want is a gigantic power: one that can change your life, and make it better and more beautiful than ever. Naturally, when you know you can bring different changes to your life, you start consciously working on the changes you want and in the process, start manifesting your desires.

With this power, you can do anything you want—improve your self-confidence, become more courageous, take risks in life, strengthen your bond with loved ones, tap into your spirituality, beat procrastination so you can work hard and achieve your goals, acquire wealth and abundance, and do absolutely anything. You are genuinely a lot more powerful, potent, and amazing than you realize and acknowledge.

"Poverty hides itself in thought before it surrenders to purses." – **Khalil Gibran**

If you are not proud of your current life and state, understand that the life you are now living is one of your making. Your destiny, the universe, your environment, the people around you, and the situations you have encountered are not to blame for the life you have now.

You are constantly creating your life and as such, you are the one to blame for any unhappiness you experience: you have manifested it. Further, if you were unaware of this realization and were not conscious of your power, even then, you bear all the blame.

If you are currently enduring a lot of pain, it is your fault. If you find it difficult to make ends meet, you are responsible for that mess. If you are nowhere near fulfilling your goals, you are answerable for that since YOU are the one creating your life and if you want to improve it, it is about time you become accountable for that.

"When you assume responsibility for what you experience and share what you experience in a spirit of companionship, this is the same as forgiveness. When you hold someone responsible for what you experience, you lose power." **– Gary Zukav**

The sooner you understand this reality, the better it is for you. When you genuinely understand, accept, and acknowledge this fact, the sooner you will start taking authority of your life. Instead of feeling like a victim burdened by problems you do not know how to fix, you will move to a role of power, authority, and strength because you now know the power lies within your mind. When you make peace with this realization, you understand that you are the one who needs to step on to the driving seat of your life's car and steer it in the right direction. This realization helps to make slow and positive changes that help you accomplish the many, amazing milestones that contribute towards creating a good life.

How can you consciously create the life you desire? The answer is simple: *through your thoughts and beliefs.* We are indeed the mirrors of our beliefs and thoughts. Whatever we think, we reflect. If you think positively, nurture the right beliefs, and constantly reinforce them, you will carve for yourself an amazing life. How do positive thoughts help us manifest a good life? That is courtesy of the 'Law of Attraction.'

Understanding the Law of Attraction and its Power

"The Law of Attraction states that whatever you focus on, think about, read about, and talk about intensely, you're going to attract more of into your life." – **Jack Canfield**

The 'Law of Attraction' is a law that governs our life. The law states you draw towards you and manifest whatever you focus on. If you are focusing on something positive, you will draw positive experiences towards you. However, if your focus lies on something negative, you will only attract negative experiences and opportunities towards you.

For instance, if you have constant fears regarding the business you recently started, if you constantly think of how it is going to fail, and do not feel confident about its success, you will eventually draw failure towards you. Fear is a negative emotion and if you constantly feed your mind fear related thoughts, you will solely act and behave according to this emotion: forcing you to feel limited, unconfident, and unhappy. In turn, you will attract negative experiences and opportunities towards you – hindering you from utilizing your unlimited potential.

The law of attraction channels the power of your mind to translate whatever lies in your thoughts. As you now know, your thoughts and beliefs help you create your reality; the law of attraction (LOA) materializes this power. Knowingly or unknowingly, we are constantly using the power of the LOA. In most instances, we are unaware of what we are thinking. Often times, we are ruminating on unhealthy thoughts and painful memories without realizing the results this rumination will yield. If we go through a painful incident, instead of letting it go, we keep thinking about it repeatedly, and we end up feeling stressed, anxious, depressed, and even miserable.

Similarly, when we make mistakes, we hold on to them and keep lamenting instead of forgiving ourselves and learning from those setbacks. Because we keep thinking of what went wrong, we fail to focus on how we can fix the issues in the present. Since negative elements occupy our thoughts, we only attract negativity towards ourselves.

As you can see, your thoughts attract unhealthy, undesirable, and meaningless things towards you. If your life is full of unwanted elements, terrible situations, experiences, and debilitating people, it is because of your thoughts and beliefs. Since you are not making good use of the LOA, it is not benefitting you.

"Everything you want is out there waiting for you to ask. Everything you want also wants you. But you have to take action to get it." – **Jack Canfield**

As the quote above states, to make the LOA work for you, you have to take action. To take the right action, you must know how you manifest your reality.

How to Manifest Your Reality

"The predominant thought or the mental attitude is the magnet, and the law is that like attracts like. Consequently, the mental attitude will invariably attract such conditions as to correspond to its nature."–
Charles Haanel

To make LOA work for you, there are a few things you must understand and acknowledge.

- Firstly, understand you are manifesting your reality all the time: you are creating every moment of your life. You create the joy you experience in one moment followed by the tears you shed in the other. How is that possible you may ask? Well, to understand that, ask yourself this simple question: *Do you ever stop thinking?* The answer is likely to be 'no'. If you cannot stop thinking and are constantly thinking of one thing or another, it means you are incessantly creating your reality. You are not a sitting duck at what destiny has in store for you; instead, you are unconsciously creating your own destiny. Every thought you create and all the beliefs powered by your thoughts play a monumental role in materializing your reality. If you are constantly thinking about how unlucky you are, it is no wonder you feel unlucky and attract experiences that strengthen this belief. However, if you focus on fulfilling your dream, a dream such as becoming a national heavyweight champion, you will undoubtedly bring this goal closer to you and actualize it.

- Secondly, you must understand that you are a powerful, spiritual being. You, when connected to the Universal Mind, create your reality and in turn, the reality of the world. You have a power and ability so unique and brilliant that if used correctly, can help you live an empowered, successful, and extraordinary life. The direction you want to steer your life in is a choice that lies within your hands: **you are responsible and accountable for this decision.**

- Once you have settled on the two truths stated above, you must clarify what you want to manifest. To create everything you want, need, and desire, it is important to be clear on all those things. Figure out what you desire the most in different areas of your life—health, appearance, relationships, love, wealth, fitness, spirituality, abundance, and religion— then actively work to manifest all of that.

- Actively working for what you want to manifest means you think positive so you bring positive experiences toward you. Secondly, you must visualize what you desire so you make your mind focus on what you want. Visualization is a tool that helps you concentrate on the bigger picture and makes your subconscious mind aware of your goals. The more focused you are on your goals, the more you think about them. When you constantly think about something, it turns into your belief and at this point, you already know what strong beliefs can do for you.

- Once you think in the right direction and visualize your aim, start being indifferent to it. Make it a constant in your life by repeatedly thinking of it. Once you develop a habit of thinking a certain way, you consciously and unconsciously create that reality. That is when you harness the full power of the LOA.

5 Keys to Manifestation

Here are the five keys to manifestation you need to be aware of and accept to become the true master of your life.

You Can Manifest Anything: Always remember that you can manifest whatever you want: anything. Be it a quality, trait, physical or emotional quality, materialistic goal, or anything else in the world: **you can manifest it all**. As the famous quote by Charles Haanel states, *"There is no limit to what this law can do for you; dare to believe in your own ideal; think of the ideal as an already accomplished fact."*

Be Clear About What You Want and Be Determined To Get It: Before you embark on the journey of manifesting any goal, ensure you are clear about whether or not you truly want it in your life. For instance, if you desire to be a millionaire, be clear about it. Ask yourself several times whether or not being a millionaire is your heart's true desire. Give yourself plenty of time to think a goal through before you start manifesting it. This helps you know your true wants, needs, desires, which in turn makes you more determined about your goals.

Analyze Your Goal Several Times: Before pursuing the manifestation of a certain goal, analyze it as many times as possible. What seems to be a lucrative or desirable goal at one time may be meaningless once you turn it into reality. For instance, you may feel you want wealth, but after you acquire it, you may find out that what you craved for was loved ones: people you could share your life with. To make sure you do not go chasing the wrong goal or idea, assess it several times, and analyze it in great depth to ensure it is your true want or need.

Think In Terms Of True Needs: Always think in terms of your true, genuine needs and stop pursuing goals that help satisfy your greed or ego. Pay close attention to your ultimate and deepest desires and needs and focus on manifesting them. For instance, you may feel you crave wealth, but when you analyze your deepest needs, you may realize what you want is to increase your self-confidence so you can go after your dreams and believe in yourself. Hence, make sure you clearly know your genuine needs and work on manifesting them.

Become One With The Universal Mind: Lastly, acknowledge and accept the fact that you are a creator who works in coordination with the Universal Mind. The sooner you accept this reality, the quicker you will align your mind with the Universal Mind and will start to harness its power.

These 5 keys are what you need to understand and apply in your routine life to become the true creator of your destiny. Let us see how you can apply these 5 keys.

How to Apply the 5 Keys of Manifestation

"Man, alone, has the power to transform his thoughts into physical reality; man, alone, can dream and make his dreams come true."
– Napoleon Hill

Here is how you can use your ultimate power of belief to create a beautiful reality for yourself.

Step 1: Know Your Deepest and Genuine Desires

"Desire is the starting point of all achievement, not a hope, not a wish, but a keen pulsating desire which transcends everything." **– Napoleon Hill**

The first step to manifesting an objective is to know it. If you do not know what you want, if you are unaware of what you desire, and if you do not understand your heart's genuine needs and requirements, you cannot manifest the right things.

Your true desire and needs are the starting point of your journey to manifestation. When you know your deepest and truest needs, you set out on a journey to manifest them and create for yourself a reality you feel connected to; a reality you feel happy about. To figure out your desires, do the following:

- Find a comfortable, quiet spot, and along with your journal and a pen, get settled in it.

- Get comfortable and when you feel relaxed, think of something you really want to create in yourself or in your life. If too many things pop up, pick one you desire the most at this moment and focus on it.

- To figure out your desires, take as much time as you need, or to pick a desire you truly want to cultivate. There is no hurry; please go slow so you work on manifesting the right thing.

- Once you settle on a particular object or objective, contemplate on your desire and figure out its role, importance, and need in your life. Ponder on what benefit that goal or object will bring to you: how will it make your life comfortable, happy, or meaningful? Ask yourself questions such as

"Why do I need this thing in my life?"

"What goal will I achieve by cultivating this thing?"

"How will this improve my life?"

"How will this goal make my life more meaningful?"

"Is it something I really need or is it a desire that will fade away after a while?"

- Take enough time on this stage so you really know how whatever you want to manifest shall help you in life and how it will help you reach the point you want to be in. These questions help you understand whether a specific desire is your genuine need. As stated before, you must focus on your genuine needs so you cultivate a reality that can truly enhance your life experience.

- Write down whatever answers you get and ponder on them for hours, days, or even weeks—as long as it takes to figure out your true needs.

- Once you have settled on what you need and want to create, write it down in bold on a fresh page and tell yourself you have already achieved that goal. For instance, if you desire to be in a healthy, loving relationship with your spouse and want to turn your existing strained relationship into a beautiful, passionate, and meaningful one, create suggestions like "I am in a healthy, loving and beautiful relationship with my spouse" or other similar suggestions.

- Chant them frequently to make your mind believe you have indeed achieved all of that. To harness the power of your mind, you must do this repeatedly: your mind focuses better on things you repeatedly say to it. In addition, when you affirm something to your mind, you declare it to be the ultimate truth; whatever your mind perceives as true, it turns into belief.

Naturally, when you have a strong belief, it will help you bring positive experiences towards you and will allow you to channelize the power of the Universal Mind to materialize your goal.

Go through these steps until you know your truest desire and make sure you go slow and steady. You are the one who is going to live with the reality you create and therefore, you must create something you truly want.

After going through this step, it is time to take necessary action, which is the second step.

Step 2: Take Necessary Action

The LOA and the Universal Mind have unimaginable power and while your beliefs can help you harness and use them to materialize your desires, for that to happen, you must take the necessary and right actions.

"To accomplish great things, we must not only act but also dream; not only plan but also believe." – **Anatole France**

The quote above states the 4 elements you need to manifest any of your desires:

dreaming, **taking action**, **believing,** and **planning**. You must dream to know your desires and stay focused on the bigger picture, and you must believe in those dreams to create powerful thoughts that can bring similar, positive experiences and opportunities toward you. However, you must also plan on how to make those dreams come true and then take the right action to fulfill that plan and actualize your wishes. Without acting, you can never fulfill your dreams. Even if you have the most amazing and healthiest beliefs in the world, but fail to take action, you will never make them work.

After you have settled on a desire you would like to manifest, your next job is to build an action plan that can help you fulfill that goal and objectify it. Taking positive actions towards your goal is exactly what helps you manifest it.

Your action plan is a detailed strategy that provides you a series of steps/actions you need to take consistently to move towards your goals. When you consistently take positive action, your abilities become enhanced, and when you get better at doing something, it becomes much easier to manifest.

For instance, if your deepest desire is to win a swimming gold at the Olympics, you will have to take the right action to achieve this goal. Your action plan could comprise of steps such as 'polish your swimming skills', 'participate in competitions at state level to become recognized at the national level', 'win national and international competitions to prove your worth', 'get selected for the Olympics team from your country' and so on. When you consistently practice all these steps, your swimming skills and talents will automatically enhance themselves, and will help you eventually manifest your goal and turn it into reality.

Your beliefs play a monumental role in this process: they allow you to put faith in your capabilities and trust yourself to achieve all you want. They also help you trust that the universe will always be by your side, considering that you strongly believe in its power. Once you believe in yourself, the

Universal Mind, and its power, you begin to harness it and use it to fulfill each step stated in your plan of action. Your beliefs combined with your positive actions help you create a reality that is beyond your imagination. With these two tools, you can achieve even the most difficult and seemingly impossible goals.

After identifying your desire, the one you want to manifest, make a thorough plan of action detailing how you intend to actualize it. To do this, identify all the little to big steps and milestones you must take to move closer to your goal. This will be overwhelming at the start, but it does not have to be that way: to simplify things, just break each step into lots of bite-sized pieces. When you are aware of every tiny step you need to take to complete a task, it stops haunting you and you begin to stop perceiving it as a challenge because you know you can complete it. Combine all the puzzle pieces and you will have your plan of action in front of you.

Now your job is to start working on your plan of action so you can use it to create your reality. Before you do that, you must go through one more step: **cultivate gratitude.**

Step 3: Cultivate Gratitude for Your Desires and Goals

"Gratitude opens the door to the power, the wisdom, and the creativity of the universe. You open the door through gratitude." –
Deepak Chopra

Gratitude is indeed a powerful emotion that can help you harness the full power of the Universal Mind. Having gratitude means being thankful for all you have and considering everything in your life a blessing.

When you cultivate gratitude, you learn to see everything through an optimistic lens and train yourself to be thankful for all the blessings in your life. Instead of complaining for things you do not have, you shift your focus on everything bestowed upon you and consider yourself 100% lucky.

By doing this, you radiate a positive energy that conveys a message of appreciation to the universe. It lets the universe know that you acknowledge and appreciate all it has given you and accept its infinite power. It also gives the Universal Mind the message that you are aware of its amazing potential and know nothing in this world can happen without its consent. Naturally, when you nurture such beliefs, you feel more positive, which strengthens your faith that nothing wrong will happen as long as you are in harmony with the Universal Mind.

When you send positive vibes into the universe, you receive positivity in return. In fact, the Universal Mind acknowledges your gratitude and helps you manifest your desires. Hence having gratitude for your desire and every blessing in your life is crucial to making the power of belief work in your favor.

By cultivating gratitude, you also learn to shun dissatisfaction and discontentment. When you focus on the things missing in your life or feel that things are not working out for you, you feel unhappy. However, by shifting your focus to your blessings, you nurture contentment and thankfulness, which gradually helps you overcome dissatisfaction and makes sure you never think or feel negatively. To open the door of the infinite power of the universe, you must cultivate gratitude.

To do that, habitually see everything around you and every situation you experience as a blessing, not as an obstacle. If you get up to drink water, thank the universe for giving you access to clean drinking water and acknowledge the plight of those who do not have hygienic water to drink.

If you are getting ready for work, pay your gratitude for having clean clothes to wear and for having the strength and health to do your work on your own instead of relying on someone else to do it for you. If you get stuck in a traffic jam on your way to work, instead of cursing and complaining about how bad the day is and 'prophesying' how bad it will be, be thankful for it as it gave you some time alone to listen to your favorite music, and think about your life, or that it may have saved you from an accident.

Whatever you do and experience, make sure to pick out one or more positives about that thing or from that situation and pay your gratitude to the universe for that blessing. It will take a while to nurture this habit, but once you develop it, you will find it easy to be thankful and positive at all times. This will help strengthen your healthy beliefs and use them together with the power of the Universal Mind to materialize all your desires.

As you can see, ultimately, you are in control of your life and you are responsible for harnessing the power of your mind to create a life of your choosing.

Now that you know how you create beliefs, and how beliefs help you manifest your reality, let us move on to discussing how to develop and nurture the right thoughts so you think positive and manifest a beautiful reality for yourself.

Part 2

Shift Your Thoughts

"The pleasantest things in the world are pleasant thoughts: and the great art of life is to have as many of them as possible."
– **Montaigne**

Indeed, good thoughts are pleasant and if you have them in surplus, your life will be nothing but blissful. Your current life and emotional state are the offspring of your thoughts: **cultivate the bad thoughts and your life will be miserable; nurture good thoughts and your life will be amazing**.

To make your life meaningful, empowered, peaceful, and successful, and to manifest every single genuine desire you have, shifting the direction of your thoughts from negative to positive is **critical**. You cannot move forward and bid adieu to your miseries unless you vow to change your thoughts and then exert effort to improving them. This part of the book focuses entirely on this shift and helps you implement it.

Let us find out how you can train your mind to think in the right direction.

Chapter 4

Understand This: Thoughts Lay the Foundation for Your Beliefs

"You are today where your thoughts have brought you; you will be tomorrow where your thoughts take you." - **James Allen**

We have already learned that your thoughts shape your life. Yes, strong beliefs hugely contribute to your current state in life, but as you should know by now, they too depend on your thoughts and as such, your thoughts are the smallest but most fundamental building blocks of your life. They are similar to the cells in your body; they (millions of them) make up different tissues, muscles, and organs and are responsible for your well-being. When an infection ravages your cells and you fail to take care of it on time, that infection affects your whole body and if the force of the infection becomes overpowering, they succumb to it.

Similarly, your thoughts serve as the many tiny bricks that when laid together, form the beliefs that build your life. If you nurture a wrong thought, it will slowly poison your other thoughts, and in turn, will result in the formation of a wrong, unhealthy, and unconstructive belief. When you have many unconstructive beliefs, they spew their venom into your life: creating experiences and situations you do not want.

As you can see, your thoughts are the seeds from which your beliefs sprout; sow the right seeds and get a beautiful plant in return.

Let us talk more about this here.

Sow the Right Thoughts Now to Nurture the Right Beliefs that Yield Amazing Results

"In your hands will be placed the exact results of your thoughts; you will receive that which you earn, no more, no less. Whatever your present environment may be, you will fail, remain, or rise with your thoughts, wisdom, desire, as great as your dominant aspiration." – **James Allen**

Your thoughts are the keys that help you unlock different doors in your life that bring towards you different surprises and situations. If you fashion the right keys, you will open the right doors and those doors will, in turn, lead you to unimaginably amazing opportunities and experiences.

To live a life full of amazing experiences, you first must work on your thoughts. Beliefs come after that. You need to think positive so you feel positive and then act positive. When you think positively and replace negative, debilitating thoughts with positive and healthier ones, you slowly build a strong, healthy, and positive mindset. This mindset encourages you to think outside the box, look for the good in even the worst-case scenarios, and helps you continue believing in yourself.

This mindset helps you shape profound, progressive, and positive beliefs that consequently build your entire life. With those beliefs, you can create anything you want and not even the sky will be the limit; for you will have harnessed the power of the Universal Mind. Hence, to achieve that, the first thing you need to do is to understand the power of your thoughts so you can then work on improving them.

Let us see how you can bring the shift from negative thinking to positive thinking in the next chapter.

Chapter 5
Think Big

"Think big, believe big, act big, and the results will be big." – **Anonymous**

Once you understand the role your thoughts play in creating your life, you need to move on to thinking big and positive. Since you must think anyway, why not think, and dream **big**.

This statement also happens to be similar to one of Donald Trump's quotes that states, *"If you're going to be thinking anything, you might as well think big."* Trump is undoubtedly one of the most fearless and headstrong people who has used big and positive thinking to manifest a reality that is just as grand as he is.

His ideas, approach to life, and methodologies may not be accepted and appreciated by all, but that is not what we are discussing here. The point we are trying to highlight is that this man created his ideal reality by believing in himself and never giving up. He was once in a $9 billion debt, which is gigantic and completely unbearable for many of us. Even then, this man stayed true to his beliefs, did not give up on himself, survived that loss, and paved his way back to success by getting out of the debt and creating a net worth of around $4 billion.

If he did not think big or believe in himself, he could have never gotten out of that dark pit. The lesson you need to pick out of this story is "to think big and believe in yourself no matter what", because that is how you can manifest the life you want live.

Let us see how thinking big helps you harness the power of the universe and how you can develop the ability to think big.

Bigger and Better Thoughts Yield Bigger and Better Results

"Big thinking precedes great achievement."
– Wilferd A. Peterson

You already know that whatever you think, you attract similar things towards yourself, which means if you think small and do not dare to dream big, you are likely to bring only small and mediocre things and opportunities into your life. If you want to be a millionaire, but you think that will not be possible and thusly, you only dream of earning about $1,000 a month because you think you can easily achieve that goal, that is exactly what you will get: a $1,000 each month. What you think, you reap; if you think small, you will reap small too.

To get bigger and better results in life, and to multiply your happiness by infinity, you must be courageous enough and think in terms of bigger goals and dreams. It takes a lot of courage to think big because thinking big requires you to believe in yourself, and believing does not come easy to many of us. However, if you are courageous and do train your mind to think big, you will eventually create an amazing reality that will be far better than what you envisaged.

When you think big, you train your mind to constantly think that way. If you imagine yourself achieving big goals and living an amazing life—whichever way you define an amazing life—you slowly guide your mind to produce similar thoughts that attract similar opportunities and experiences towards: helping you create your ideal reality.

In addition, since your subconscious cannot distinguish between what is real and what is imaginary, when you dream big, you convey to it the message that 'the particular dream/thought' is true. When your subconscious accepts something as true, it shifts your focus in that direction and makes you concentrate more on that object. Naturally, when your focus on something increases, you look for ways to accomplish it and turn that dream into your reality.

By simply building the habit of thinking big, you can manifest all your hopes and wishes. Well, this does not mean that to create a good life for yourself, you must only think of becoming a billionaire. Thinking big does not imply you need to think in terms of creating heaps of money and achieving financial success. Thinking big is thinking of the best possible scenario relevant to your goal and genuine desires.

If your desire is to find your soul mate, think of having found the best mate in the world and having found for yourself a partner who loves you more than anything in the world: someone who is extremely passionate about you and someone you are head over heels in love with. Do not merely imagine yourself being in a relationship with a good person.

Similarly, if you desire to start a charitable organization that works for the rights of the transgender community, an organization that helps them attain their basic rights, do not think of having started one small organization that helps a few transgender people in your area. Instead, imagine of having started a chain of such organizations that are now doing great work for the transgender community in the entire country and spreading to other parts of the world.

When you think of achieving your genuine desire, you need to think achieving big goals and dreams. Your genuine desire can be absolutely anything in the world: it need not focus on creating monetary wealth and abundance only. Whatever you think of, you

MUST only THINK BIG! Ensure **your desire is 100% genuine and your beliefs about it are 100% authentic, and then think big. When your desires come from love and sincerity, and you then use the power of thinking big**, **nothing** can stop you from achieving them.

When you have genuine desires you feel thankful for, you believe in yourself, and the universe starts to work in your favor; when the Universal Mind showers its favor on you, you are bound to become successful.

Thinking Big is not Synonymous to Daydreaming

Thinking big does not mean to resorting to daydreaming and doing nothing all day. Thinking big does not mean you should build castles in the air and let them vanish without taking action. Thinking big means dreaming big and visualizing whatever you think of so you can expand the horizons of your mind and force it to think outside the box - you do not just think of desires; you think of how you will achieve them too.

When you think of becoming a successful writer, you also think of **how** you can become one; this trains your mind to think of ways to help you achieve your goals. This quality is one you need to accomplish your dreams: broaden your horizons so you can find solutions to your problems and make your dreams your reality.

When you build the habit of thinking big, your mind brings to your awareness many hacks, techniques, methods and ideas that lend you a hand in achieving your goals at whatever pace you desire. People who achieve great success and who accomplish their set goals quickly do so thanks to their ability to think big and visualize what they want. Since they have the ability to think big, they quickly find ways to manifest their dreams and make sure to work on them to materialize them. This is the main difference between those who accomplish their goals fast and make the most of their time, and those who stay stagnant in one position for years.

Yes, thinking big greatly influences your time management skills. If you think big and constantly visualize yourself achieving your goals, you force your mind to think of ways to implement these goals, and you begin to act.

Because you want great results fast, you think of great ways to make the most of your time so you can use it effectively and efficiently to yield amazing results. This helps you move closer to your goals quickly and successfully. As Tony Robbins once stated, *"Once you have mastered time, you will understand how true it is that most people over-estimate what they can accomplish in a year, and underestimate what they could achieve in a decade."*

As you can see, by simply thinking big, you can achieve all you want - thinking big makes you believe in yourself; this helps you grow your potential. When you think small, you underestimate your potential. You tell yourself that performing greatness is not achievable and that you will never accomplish your dreams. This will hinder you from achieving the profound success you know you are meant for.

When you lower your goals to a 'mediocre' or 'easily achievable' level, you lower your standards, your beliefs, your expectations, and in turn, your outcomes. To make sure you do not sabotage your life by doing that, **start thinking big**.

Let us see the different ingredients you need to use to nurture the habit of thinking big and positive.

1: Think Courageously

"Every single second is an opportunity to change your life because in any moment, you can change the way you feel." –
Rhonda Byrne

Indeed. Every moment you experience is an opportunity to transform your life; for that to happen, you must start thinking fearlessly and courageously. Thinking fearlessly means you stop limiting yourself. When you think bravely, you understand that there is no limit to how much you can achieve and nothing can stop you from accomplishing your dreams.

Courageous thinking is what changes 'impossible' to 'possible'; when you think big and boldly, you stop confining yourself to limits. If you want to achieve something, you embark on the journey of materializing it no matter what. Instead of thinking "this goal is not achievable," you look for opportunities and methods that make it doable.

When Stephen King decided to pursue his passion for writing, he faced massive rejection. Publishers rejected his novel a number of times and he nearly gave up hope in himself, which is when his wife encouraged him to keep thinking big. She gave him a nudge forward and stimulated his motivation. Her encouragement helped him become fearless, which eventually made him complete his novel 'Carrie' and get it published. The novel was a success and since its publication, Stephen King never looked back.

This is just one example of an accomplished person who dared to think big and fearless, and as a result, received great outcomes. You will find many other examples of people like Stephen King who dared to believe in themselves, which is how they accomplished their success. One of these people is Katy Perry. While we are all aware of her successes, many of us do not know the struggles she encountered to prove her worth. Katy Perry began her music career early when she dropped out of school while still a freshman. In 2001, she released her very first album, a big commercial flop. The record company she had signed on terminated the contract. Despite this failure, Perry never gave up; she never stopped thinking fearlessly. She was courageous and determined to achieve her goals, so she switched her focus from gospel music to pop singing and pursued it. She again experienced a few more setbacks as none of the deals she signed with different companies emerged successful. Even then, she did not give up on herself; she pursued her passion for music and eventually released her hit single 'I Kissed a Girl' that became a massive hit and paved way for Perry's success. Had Perry stopped thinking big and believing in herself, she would have never accomplished the success she is enjoying today.

How to Think Bravely

Fearless thinking is what helped Stephen King, Katy Perry, and many others like them carve their names in the world, and it can do the same for you. Here is how you can train yourself to think big and fearlessly.

Eliminate Impossible from Your Life: Firstly, eliminate the term 'impossible' from your mind, vocabulary, and life. Impossible is a term that limits the potential of your mind and makes you think you are incapable of achieving your desires. To let go of such thoughts and beliefs, you must purge the word impossible from your mind's dictionary. Instead of thinking that achieving your goals is not possible, make them possible by changing 'impossible' to 'I am possible.' Whenever you embark on a journey to achieve a certain desire or set a goal for yourself, write

'This is possible' next to that goal and keep telling yourself how you will achieve it.

Find Reasons Why You Can Achieve a Goal: Thinking that achieving a goal is possible can often be difficult. To compel your mind to believe you can and will achieve it, identify all the reasons why you can accomplish a goal and focus on them. People who fail to achieve their dreams focus on all the reasons why they cannot fulfill their goals.

To differentiate yourself and never let go of your dreams, focus on the reasons why you can and eventually will become successful. Think of your strengths and your passion for a certain goal and use that information to find reasons why you can accomplish it. For instance, if you want to become a published writer, tell yourself you can do it because you are an excellent writer, have been writing articles for 5 years, and have an incredible drive to make your mark on the industry.

These reasons will stimulate you to pursue your desire and ultimately accomplish it. Write those reasons in your journal; this will solidify them and remind you of your 'whys' for pursing a specific desire.

See Problems as Opportunities and Challenges: Thirdly, stop perceiving problems as failures. Obstacles appear as obstacles only when you perceive them as difficulties and obstructions. The situation is not the problem; your perception of it is. The problem lies within you: your limiting mindset forces you to see that situation/event/issue as a problem and not as an opportunity to grow.

If you shift your outlook and change the way you see it, you will start perceiving that same problem as an opportunity to help you grow, instead of an issue that limits your potential. As Wally Amos once said, *"Nothing is an obstacle unless you say it is."* So, stop viewing the different difficulties in your life as obstructions and start seeing them as growth opportunities.

To build that outlook, always look for the good in a situation/event/issue you deem problematic. If you aspire to become a novelist, but your first published novel does not garner much attention and success, instead of sulking, find out why it did not become a commercial hit and improve on those areas. Similarly, look for ways to get better after each challenge so you can improve your skill and make yourself successful.

By adopting this outlook, you will easily start moving past your obstacles and closer to your goals. Also, whenever you face an obstacle, remind yourself of this quote by Chuck Norris, *"A lot of people give up just before they're about to make it. You know, you never know when that next obstacle is going to be the last one."*

You do not know if that one obstacle is the last in the line of your share of challenges in this life and might be the one that opens the door to your success. Therefore, never stop fighting, and you will emerge more successful, braver, and more amazing than ever before.

In addition to thinking fearlessly, practice visualization. This is yet another tactic to think big.

2: Visualize Your Desires

"The more light you allow within you, the brighter the world you live in will be." –
Shakti Gawain

You have a bright power within you, and with the power of visualization, you can make that light inside you brighter than it has ever been. Visualizing something means seeing something happening to you right now.

If you want to visualize yourself as a happy person who is in an amazing relationship with the love of his/her life and who has a beautiful child to celebrate that love for his partner/spouse, you need to imagine yourself living a happy, meaningful life with your soul mate and raising a baby together. Using imagery and sounds, you need to imagine that scenario and involve yourself in it so you feel as if you are actually living it.

This practice adds value to your thoughts and strengthens them. At its most basic level, visualization is a technique that compels your subconscious to accept a goal as the ultimate truth so it focuses more on it and drives you to pursue it.

This mental rehearsal of visualizing your goals also gives you a taste of your accomplishment. When you get that enjoyable taste, you become compelled to pursue your goal. As such, visualization serves as an impetus that makes you chase your desires and eventually fulfill them. To make the magic of visualization work for you, do the following.

How to Practice Visualization

"Visualize the most amazing life imaginable to you. Close your eyes and see it clearly. Then hold the vision for as long as you can. Now place the vision in God's hands and consider it done." – Marianne Williamson

This quote by Marianne Williamson describes how to exercise visualization. Here is the detailed breakdown of that quote as well as the procedure you need to follow to exercise this practice.

1. For a little while, sit somewhere quiet and peaceful.

2. Close your eyes and think of your ultimate desire or any desire you would like to manifest right now or in the near future.

3. Focus completely on that desire and for a few minutes, think only of it.

4. Now start visualizing yourself achieving that goal. If you desire to have children or to have a mansion of your own, visualize yourself accomplishing these goals. Think of yourself being a happy and proud parent, having two or as many kids as you want, and happily raising them in a healthy, loving environment you have built for them. If your goal is to have a mansion, imagine of having eventually created plenty of wealth that has allowed you to purchase a mansion and you are finally signing the deal. What sounds do you hear when you visualize that scene? What colors can you see? What textures can you feel and touch? Are there any odors you can smell? Focusing on these

things will engage your senses in the visualization. This increases your engagement in the imagination and makes it feel alive.

5. Keep visualizing that scenario for a while—20 or more minutes is good.

6. When you are ready to finish the session, open your eyes and take as much time as you need to absorb the feelings bubbling inside you.

7. Write down all you saw—this helps you remember your goal clearly, which makes your visualization vivid and easier to explore. Maybe you saw something that gave you a clue about any other desire. This helps you better understand yourself and the way you want to fulfill your goals.

Exercise this practice daily for as many times as you like and soon enough, you will start thinking bigger and better than ever. In addition, you will feel motivated enough to work on your goals and make them a reality. As you work on this strategy, make sure to cultivate the habit of being a creative thinker.

3: Become a Creative Thinker

Creativity is the ability to think differently and see outside the box. This ability allows you to see things from a different perspective. When you have a creative mind, you begin perceiving problems as opportunities. When others see a closed door, you see hope, light, and possibilities all around you simply because you have the power to put a creative spin on everything and see things through different lenses.

To become a positive thinker who never loses sight of his/her goals, someone capable of manifesting his/her desires, you must become creative. To be innovative, never stop dreaming; let your dreams fan the burning flames of your desires so they keep growing bigger and higher.

Every night before going to bed, think of your desires and think of how you can achieve them efficiently. If you plan to become a musician and do not know how to polish your drumming and singing skills without enrolling into a music school, think of ways you can accomplish that goal on a budget e.g. watching tutorials on YouTube for instance. Similarly, whenever thinking of your goal and especially while visualizing it, put your creative cap on.

Moreover, think of how you would manifest your desires if everything goes against you and you receive no opportunity to fulfill your goal. Think of the different paths you would take to actualize your goal if everywhere you stepped on were a dead end. What would you do then? What would you do to move closer to your goal? This practice helps you reframe different problems and your situation. It helps you find creative fixes for any issues you have in your life. To enhance your creative ability, make sure you write down those solutions and then analyze them from different angles.

To think big, practice these tactics daily. To keep growing your big dreams, remember to believe in yourself.

Never Stop Believing in Yourself

Even if you do everything discussed above but fail to believe in yourself, you will never manifest your reality or achieve what you genuinely desire. To magnify your ability to think big, positively, and creatively, you must always believe in yourself.

"Life can be much broader once you discover one single fact, and that is: everything around you that you call life was made up by people that were not smarter than you. You can change it, you can influence it; you can build things other people can use. Once you learn that, you will never be the same again" – **Steve Jobs**

Steve Job's profound quote beautifully describes the power of believing in yourself and having immense faith and trust in your capabilities. To multiply your positive thoughts and to increase their magnitude, it is important that you learn how to increase their size.

For that, always be sincere with yourself about your desires. Your desires must be very genuine and must only sprout from the positive beliefs that come from your heart. For that, you need self-realization, which means you need to know who you are and be painfully aware of yourself. To achieve self-realization, spend quality time with yourself every single day and focus deeply on whom you are, what you want in life, and the purpose you want to fulfill.

The more you understand yourself, the better insight you gain into your thoughts and desires, which in turn helps you understand your genuine needs and then work hard to manifest them. When you are aware of your sincere and authentic desires and needs, you begin to realize which way you must direct your thoughts. This helps you think big and break the shackles of limiting self-talk, which helps you develop a growth mindset that pushes you to dream big and pursue those dreams.

To keep reinforcing your growth mindset, also crucially important is decluttering your mind of the meaningless, unconstructive, negative, and extra thoughts. The next chapter talks about this in detail.

Chapter 6

Declutter Your Mind

"Clutter is not just in your home, attic, garage, or office. Clutter is also in your mind and distracts you from the amazing things you need to do to achieve much success." – **Katrina Mayer**

Clutter is anything that creates a mess within yourself or your mind and distracts you from the crucially important aspects of your life. As physical clutter adds chaos to your house/workplace and weakens your focus, mental clutter does the same to your mind.

If you want to focus on the good and positive things, want to be build strong, optimistic, and healthy beliefs, and want to create a beautiful life for yourself and those you love, it is time you realize the harms of mental clutter and work on getting rid of it.

Let us find out what mental clutter is, how it spews venom in your life, and how you can eliminate it.

Understanding Mental Clutter and its Harms

For a minute, think you intend to complete an important report today and are determined to work on it as soon as you sit down. You enter your workplace intending to work on your project, but instead you become sidetracked by the piles of files lying aimlessly on the floor and your table. Instead of starting work on the report, you start organizing those files.

Before you are through with that task, you remember you were supposed to send an email to a client today so you start to search for an important and relevant document you need to send the email. However, since your office is in chaos, you cannot find that document. Before you can find that document, something else distracts you; one thing leads to another and before you realize, you waste the entire day doing nothing meaningful.

This is what physical clutter does to you and your life: it makes it chaotic, unorganized, and unsuccessful. The effects of mental clutter are just as bad. Mental clutter refers to all the unwanted, debilitating, and unhealthy thoughts that weaken your confidence, pollute your mind, and sidetrack you from your meaningful and genuine desires.

"Clutter is not just the stuff on your floor- it's anything that stands between you and the life you want to be living." – **Peter Walsh**

This quote by Peter Walsh could not be any truer. Clutter is indeed anything that keeps you from living the life you desire. Physical clutter definitely disturbs your life and makes things messy for you. How does mental clutter do that? Here is how.

How Mental Clutter Wreaks Your Life

We can break down mental clutter into the following elements. Here is how all these elements disturb you and decrease your chances of manifesting the reality you desire.

Negative Thoughts: These are all the unhealthy, unconstructive, and negative thoughts that make you feel incompetent, incapable, and weak. Such thoughts lower your self-esteem, causing you to devalue yourself and debilitate your self-confidence.

Naturally, when you are in low spirits, you find it difficult to ruminate on strong, empowering thoughts, and believe in yourself. This is one way through which negative thoughts weaken your self-belief, thus keeping you from investing in healthy beliefs that can help you harness your limitless power.

Further, such thoughts keep you too focused on what happened, and too concerned about what may happen; making you completely oblivious to everything that is happening right now. Naturally, when you do not live in your present, you find it difficult to cultivate gratitude, which is a major requirement for manifesting your genuine desires.

Extra, Meaningless Thoughts: These are all the thoughts about things, people, ideas or anything that does not mean much to you. Thoughts about extra, meaningless things only do you harm; they take your attention away from meaningful things, and leave less room for purposeful thoughts. For instance, if you are involved in a number of activities you do not like or enjoy, you will obviously think about them. This fills up your mind with meaningless thoughts that make it difficult for you to think of meaningful things because whenever you sit to ponder on what you genuinely need, a gazillion other thoughts will bombard you and distract you from what is important.

Not only do these thoughts increase your stress and reduce your focus, they also make concentrating on what you truly want difficult. Naturally, when your worries, problems, and meaningless things occupy your mind, you will not have any time and energy to concentrate on your true desires.

Your cluttered mind makes it nearly impossible for you to look past the clutter and seek something meaningful. It cannot find its way to the important and meaningful stuff amidst all the traffic jam of unhealthy and useless thoughts. To seek happiness, peace, and meaning in life, you must free up some space in your mind; something you can only do when you choose to declutter.

Here is how you can do that.

How to Declutter Your Mind

Decluttering your mind is paramount to building a healthy mindset that allows you to focus on everything you truly want and build empowering beliefs that unleash your inner potential.

Below are a few things you can do to declutter your mind and fill it with meaningful thoughts and empowering beliefs.

1: Be Conscious of Your Thoughts

Thinking is a spontaneous act. One second you are thinking of what to wear to work today, and the other moment you are thinking about how you lost your best friend in a car accident. How thoughts work and how one memory connects to another is seriously bizarre: a fringe science we yet to have full comprehension of.

Does this mean you have no control over your thoughts and cannot control how they affect you? The answer is multi-pronged: yes and no. No, you cannot always control the thoughts that come into your mind and to your consciousness. Yes, you can control how they affect you.

Not every thought you experience has a great influence on you. The meaning you extract from a thought, your reaction to it, and the time you ruminate on, or think about it determines how any thought influences your life. For instance, if a thought suggesting "I am useless" pops into your mind, but you do not think much of it, shake your head, avoid paying much attention, and instead, replace it with a more positive thought, you will avoid letting it affect you.

On the contrary, if you label that thought as a negative one, let it make you start thinking of all your setbacks, consider it to be a declaration of how unsuccessful you are, and spend hours thinking about it, naturally, you will feel more stressed and weaker than before. You are also likely to start focusing on unprogressive thoughts, and stop thinking of the meaningful desires you wish to manifest.

How you react to a thought plays a big role in how that thought affects you. Since thoughts enter and leave your mind all the time, and most of the time, you are unaware of the thoughts you contemplate, it is very important that you become conscious of your thought process so you can better control their influence on your life. You will never be aware of how debilitating a thought can be unless you start focusing on it deeply.

Moreover, how a thought influences you is dependent on how you perceive it. If you view a certain thought as damaging, it will sabotage your self-esteem. If you perceive another thought as depressing, it will dampen your spirits. However, if you view the same thought as positive, it will lift-up your spirits. How you see and label a thought greatly affects your well-being and the beliefs you form based on that thought.

To get rid of poisonous and meaningless thoughts from your life, you must be conscious of them. This helps you become aware of the meaning you attach to a thought, the label you place on it, and its effect on your life. One of the best ways to do that is through practicing mindfulness meditation.

Let us see what this practice is and how it can help you.

Mindfulness Based Breathing Meditation

Meditation is a practice that instills a sense of mindfulness within you and makes you more aware of yourself and everything around you. Due to our forgetful nature, it is easy for us to give in to stress-triggering and meaningless thoughts, ruminate on thoughts related to the past or future, ignore our present, not work on identifying our desires, and not know what we really want in life.

Since you are forgetful of yourself, your present, your blessings, your thoughts, and your power, and because this means you are unaware of your true self and authentic desires, you pursue the wrong things in life, which in turn causes you to place your focus on manifesting meaningless "wants". This is why you cannot build the right, empowering beliefs, and why you find it nearly impossible to tap into and use the power of the Universal Mind. You are not mindful of yourself, your needs, or your surroundings, and you do not live in the present

If you become mindful of yourself and the present moment, you will develop the ability to straighten your life for the better. Here is how mindfulness helps you.

1. You will be aware of every thought that enters and leaves your mind and thus, will become more conscious of their presence.

2. You will know the meaning you attach to a certain thought and your perceptions of it; this will help you understand its effect on your mind and well-being. For instance, if you think of how incapable you are, and you understand that this thought makes you feel inadequate, being mindful will help you stop attaching unhealthy meaning to it, and completely erase it from your mind.

3. Being conscious of your thoughts gives you the opportunity to explore and understand them better. Exploring your thoughts is the only way to find out why you think a certain way. This helps you uncover the actual reasons that result in negative thinking so you eliminate them and become happier. In addition, this helps you discover the many reasons why you cannot work on your plan of action to fulfill your genuine goals and desires. For instance, after exploring your thoughts, you may figure out that you feel inadequate because you are not as productive as you would like to be. If you beat procrastination, you can work on manifesting your true desires and increase your productivity, which will help you live a better life. Meditation helps you understand your thoughts better and gives you better insight into yourself.

4. By exploring your thoughts and yourself, you understand your deepest needs better. Naturally, when you are aware of what you need, your vision clarifies, and you find it

easy to think in the right direction and dream big.

5. Self-awareness and mindfulness also helps you get rid of negative self-talk. Self-talk is the way you speak to yourself: the inner dialogue that cultivates inside you at all times. Every time you do something, take a certain action, think of something, a two-way dialogue, or a monologue occurs in your mind. This is your self-talk; it can be negative or positive. Negative self-talk comprises of self-depreciating thoughts and suggestions that make you feel lowly of yourself, lower your self-esteem and give rise to your inner critic that leaves no opportunity to put you to shame. By being aware of yourself and your thoughts, you will understand whether you practice negative or positive self-talk, along with the reasons that lead up to them. This helps you eliminate those reasons, and get rid of negative thoughts so you can build and focus on positive ones.

6. Moreover, self-awareness is the tool you need to fully understand your genuine desires. Alongside this, mindful awareness helps you acknowledge the present moment and be happy with it instead of letting your mind lurk in the past or future. This helps cultivate gratitude, and as we have seen, gratitude is one of the key ingredients you need to manifest a good life.

Now that you know how meditation and mindfulness help declutter your mind and focus on what you want, let us see how you can practice it.

How to Practice Mindfulness Breathing Meditation

Meditation helps calm your racing mind, thus giving you more time to focus on your thoughts and analyze them.

Not only that, meditation also helps you focus your energies in the present so you enjoy the moment as it occurs. This keeps you from being judgmental of a thought or labeling it as good or bad. Naturally, when you do not label a thought, you stop seeing it as unhealthy or negative and instead, perceive it as a simple thought that will leave your mind as soon as it enters it. This allows you to view thoughts as temporary energies that are bound to occur and vanish.

When you become aware of this fact - the fact that you have control over how your thoughts influence you - and if you stop associating negativity to any of your thoughts, they will stop impacting you and eventually, you will begin seeing them for what they truly are: simple thoughts. Instead of perceiving them as elements that can sabotage your life, you shall view them as simple, meaningless thoughts; when this happens, you shall start letting them go, and continuing to live your life.

Here is how you can achieve this goal by practicing meditation regularly.

1. Sit somewhere quiet, somewhere you find it easy to relax.

2. Close your eyes and recall any happy memory that instantly cheers you up.

Think of the time you won the lottery or when your partner took you on a wonderful vacation.

3. For a few minutes, concentrate on and think of that memory, and when you feel relaxed, bring your complete attention to your breath.

4. Breathe in your natural, normal manner without deepening your breath. Just inhale through your nose and exhale through your mouth.

5. As you inhale and exhale, focus on your in-breath and out-breath and stay present with them. As you inhale, say in your mind, "I am staying with my in-breath" and focus on how you inhale, the movements the inhalation produces in your body, and how it makes you feel. If there is a fluttery sensation in your tummy, acknowledge it. If you feel your abdomen rising and falling, notice it. Similarly, stay with your out-breath and as you take it, observe it closely.

6. Keep doing this for 5 minutes. This practice helps you remain in the present and calms your mind, thus allowing you to feel and understand your inner self. With time, and as you get better at this practice, you will find it very easy to focus on the moment at hand and make the most of it. This focus also helps you concentrate better on your desires and understand them. In addition to this, you will also become more aware of your surroundings and will know how different things affect you. Self-awareness and a better understanding of how your environment influences you is critically important to a better comprehension of your needs and desires.

7. While you meditate, you may find yourself wandering off in thought; thoughts of tasks lined up next, any pending tasks, or any bad memory. If that happens to you, remember that it is perfectly normal, and you have nothing to worry about. When you wander off in thought, say, "thinking has happened." This will help you acknowledge that your attention drifted away. Next, gently bring your mind back to your breath and continue focusing. Counting your breath helps you become more aware of it, which keeps you alert.

Keep doing this for the entire length of your session and when it comes to finishing the practice, end it gently; do so by gently bringing your awareness to the real world and observing everything as if you are seeing it for the first time. This helps you see things with a different, fresh, and new perspective.

When you stand up with the intent of getting back to your routine work, do it slowly and gently. Pay close attention to everything you do as well as how you do it. If you have to pick up a glass from the table and put it in the kitchen, instead of rushing through the process, take your time doing so. Notice how the glass feels in your hand and keep telling yourself to focus only on the present task (which is to put the glass back in the kitchen) and nothing else. This simple practice helps you stay in the present at all times and become more self-aware.

Practice meditation daily for 5 to 10 minutes and then do things mindfully. After doing this for a while, you will inculcate the habit of doing so and will find yourself feeling relaxed, comfortable, and peaceful at all times. You will learn to stay present in the moment and will become more aware of how you feel and think. If you find yourself feeling distracted from your goal, you will know when it happens and will easily bring your attention back to the present.

As you get better on focusing on the moment, start meditating on your thoughts. This practice helps declutter your mind and create more space for healthy, happy thoughts. Further, this practice gives you better insight into your truest, deepest, and genuine desires.

Let us see discuss how you can meditate on your thoughts:

Meditating On Your Thoughts to Stop Judging Them and to Understand Yourself Better

To meditate on your thoughts, gain a deeper and better understanding of them, and to stop being judgmental of them, do the following:

- Calm yourself by practicing mindfulness-breathing meditation.

- When you feel relaxed, stop focusing on your breath, and let your mind loose. Let it wander and think of whatever comes to your conscious mind.

- When you observe a noticeable thought, hold on to it, and explore it deeply.

- Do not label it as a negative, bad, or unhealthy thought. If a thought states, "I am not successful and I hate myself for it," do not label that thought as a negative one. Instead, explore that thought and assess it. Rattle that thought well and find out why you feel that way. Ask yourself questions such as "Why am I unsuccessful?" "Why don't I feel good about myself?" "What can

I do to become more successful in life? Ask yourself these and other similar questions. This helps you understand the core reason why that thought emerged. Even if a certain thought is not a happy one, you can make it positive by looking for the positives attached to it. The moment you perceive any thought as a means of improving yourself, you will stop feeling bad about it. This helps you stop being judgmental of your thoughts and stop turning normal thoughts into fierce ones.

- Write the answers to the questions you ask yourself; writing your answers in your journal shall help you understand the essence of a thought.

- Once you stop viewing a thought as damaging or frightening, you stop feeling scared of, or thinking negative about it. When a thought stops bothering you, you stop holding on to it; you learn to let it go out of your system. Do this with every thought that intimidates, upsets, frustrates, or scares you and sure enough, you will start decluttering your mind of unwanted and sabotaging thoughts.

To understand your desires, practice mindfulness-breathing meditation and then focus on what you want in life. Ask yourself questions like "What do I want to do in my life?" "What is my purpose in this world and how do I plan to actualize my purpose?" "Is this what I truly want?" In addition to asking yourself these questions, focus on any of your likes, strengths, and accomplishments and to figure out your desires, ponder on them.

Make sure you do not rush through the process; take as much time as you want and need. If you feel overwhelmed at any one point, stop the practice immediately and continue it any other time you feel ready. Meditation does not aim to make you feel pressured or drained and if you feel any of these emotions, take a break, and resume your session when you feel better.

Once you figure out your true desires, focus more on them and think of them in every meditation session. This helps you imbed positive and constructive thoughts in your mind so they replace the unhealthy thoughts for good. It is very important that you exercise this technique daily for a minimum of 15 minutes—the more the better.

With time, you will get better at analyzing your thoughts, identifying your desires, and shunning the habit of labeling any thought as bad or negative. As you get better at these tasks, you will find yourself feeling more optimistic, which will in turn strengthen your belief in yourself. Naturally, when you think along the lines of happiness and optimism, your mind will brew concoctions of healthy thoughts that will give you hope and make you believe in your desires and your power.

Believing in your power and decluttering your mind is not enough. To ensure your mind stays clean of useless thoughts for good, and that you actually make good use of your positive thoughts, you also have to take action.

Take Action

To ensure all sorts of clutter stays away from your mind and life, it is crucially important that you take action on what you have learned about yourself as you practiced meditation. Here is how you can make efforts to declutter your mind and in turn, your life.

Replace Unhealthy Thoughts With Healthy Ones: When you meditate on your thoughts and spot a thought you know will wreak havoc in your life and take you on a negative journey, quickly replace it with something more positive. Even if you do not label a thought as bad and negative, you can still ponder on it and this very act can engulf you in tensions and worries. To keep that from happening, replace any debilitating thought with a kinder one.

If a thought states "I will never fulfill my dreams" and you know that holding on to this thought will make you feel terrible, change it to something nice and hopeful such as "Of course I can fulfill my dreams, but only if I work hard and believe in myself." Chant this positive suggestion several times; affirm it until your subconscious accepts it and helps you manifest your desires. Similarly, change all unhealthy thoughts to healthier, positive ones so you declutter your mind of all self-depreciating thoughts.

Get Rid of Meaningless Activities: When you meditate on your desires and explore them to figure out your true likes, interests, and passions, you find out what you want in life. This gives you better knowledge of how you plan to live. With that knowledge in hand, your job then becomes to rid yourself of everything else that does not add value to this purpose. Meaningless activities are all the endeavors and chores that do not help you fulfill your desire and instead, distract you from your goal.

Naturally, when there are such activities in your life, your mind absorbs clutter and becomes vulnerable to distractions. By eliminating those activities from your life, you make certain you stick to your desires and stay focused on them. If you have figured out that your desire is to become a violinist, and you are involved in a number of other activities that sidetrack you from violin practices, eliminate all those extra, meaningless activities so you can focus better on manifesting your desire.

Actively Pursue Your Desires: Achieving your meaningful desires is dependent on your pursuit. If you fail to pursue your dreams, you will forever remain engaged in meaningless activities and will never successfully declutter your mind.

Regular meditation helps you identify and analyze your desires. After identifying them, the next step in the process is vehemently pursuing them until they manifest in your life. You already know how to create your action plan; become determined to pursue certain desire, and then make a relevant and effective plan of action to fulfill it.

Once your plan is ready, start the implementation process; make sure you always focus on the reason WHY you want to fulfill that desire. This will help you stay focused on the bigger picture and gain a strong impetus to execute the plan.

Stop Attaching Sentiments to Overpowering Thoughts: Moreover, make a conscious effort to stop associating ill feelings with any thought. Whenever you find yourself ruminating on painful events from the past or experience overpowering concerns of the future, and you find yourself feeling stressed, overwhelmed, depressed, or experiencing any unhealthy emotion, loudly say the word 'STOP!' Say it repeatedly and within a few moments, you will stop thinking of the frustrating event/memory and will stop attaching emotions to it.

Additionally, think of a happy memory whenever you notice yourself attaching any strong or unhealthy sentiment to an overpowering thought; this will wash away the sadness. Try this technique a few times to make a habit of doing it whenever you find yourself succumbing to disturbing thoughts.

Focus Less on debilitating Thoughts: Similar to the previous tactic, this too helps you place less attention towards your debilitating thoughts. Whenever you find yourself thinking about something frustrating, divert your attention from it. If you think, "I make mistakes all the time, which is why I never fulfill my goals," just get up, go to another room, or drink a glass of water, watch a funny video online, or do a small task that helps you move even an inch closer to your goal.

The point here is to do anything that shifts your focus from the debilitating thought to something better so you stop giving too much thought and attention to that destructive thought. By doing this, you will start thinking less self-depreciating thought.

Get Rid of Extras from Your House/Workplace: Additionally, start decluttering your house and workplace so you never let your mind preoccupy itself with extra, useless thoughts. Physical clutter increases mental clutter because when you find yourself surrounded by lots of extra, meaningless, and extravagant things, you start thinking about those things, which consequently leaves little room for meaningful thoughts and instead distracts you from your genuine desires.

Deeply analyze your workplace and house and after, get rid of anything you do not need anymore, all the things you do not like, everything that is not in good working condition and is thus unusable, and everything you have spares of. This helps you fill your house and workplace with only the important things so you focus only on the important tasks.

It will take time before you start reaping benefits from these strategies but if you consistently practice them, you will definitely see amazing results. To keep amplifying and strengthening your positive beliefs, you also need to cultivate gratitude in your life. The next chapter throws light on this element.

Chapter 7

Appreciate

"Develop an attitude of gratitude and give thanks for everything that happens to you knowing that every step forward is a step toward achieving something bigger and better than your current situation." – **Brian Tracy**

Gratitude is a beautiful state of mind that if developed, helps you acknowledge all you have, feel content with it, and move forward without holding any grudges or hard feelings. Moreover, thankfulness also helps you believe in the power of the universe.

When you become cognizant of your blessings and pay gratitude to the universe for them, you let the universe know you believe in its power to do good for you. The contentment and peacefulness you experience when you are grateful helps you enjoy your life and understand that the universe will always be by your side. This increases your faith in the power of the Universal Mind, which in turn helps align your power in a similar direction.

When you are in harmony with the Universal Mind, nothing can keep you from achieving the success that is rightfully yours.

Let us deeply discuss the power of being appreciative of your blessings and the various strategies you can use to foster a grateful mind.

The Power of Gratitude

As already discussed, being grateful (gratitude) means being thankful for something. Having gratitude for yourself and your life means you acknowledge every little to big blessing and quality you have and are happy about.

By cultivating gratitude, you learn to live your life in an imoroved manner. Instead of perceiving your life as a burden, you start viewing it as a miracle; your focus shifts from everything you lack, to everything you have. This helps you become more thankful and appreciative of your loved ones, your health, your life, and your desires.

Gratitude helps you quickly acknowledge all the gifts in your life and encourages you to be kinder and compassionate towards everyone. When you practice gratitude, you start noticing the good things about your loved ones, every situation you experience, and focus more on returning the kind favor. If someone helped you out, you will not whine about how he/she could have helped you better. Instead, you will be happy that he/she helped you and you shall look for ways to return the favor to him/her.

While you're thinking that being grateful might be useless and not something that helps you become successful, you would be surprised to know that a number of accomplished people in the world swear by the importance of gratitude in their lives.

Successful people such as John Paul DeJoria, Oprah Winfrey, Timothy Ferriss, and Richard Branson are a few examples of renowned, accomplished people who consciously practice gratitude and feel indebted to this state of mind for living a healthy, happy, and content life.

To follow the footsteps of these people, you must cultivate gratitude. To do so, understand that to nurture gratitude, you do not have to practice it once or twice; instead, you need to nurture that state of mind. Yes, gratitude is a state of mind, and to live a beautiful, happy, and powerful life, you must nurture it.

Gratitude is a State of Mind

The gratitude state of mind draws upon your beliefs. To nurture gratitude, it is important that you build and then strengthen the right beliefs. To do that, you need to identify all the things you feel deeply and truly grateful for. To realize this, ask yourself "What am I thankful for?" "What makes me really happy?" "Which things/blessings add value to my life?' Ask yourself other similar questions. These questions make you more aware of your blessings and help you think positively.

When you become emotionally charged and thankful for everything you have, your emotions serve as the catalysts for extremely intense and magical transformations in your life. This transformation is often beyond everyone's imagination. While you may find this bizarre right now, ask yourself the following: do you want to live a life of abundance? Do you want to be better than you have ever been before? Do you want your wishes and desires to manifest as fast as possible? Since your answers to these questions are likely to be a 'YES,' gratitude is all you need to make it come true. Yes, like a magical elixir, gratitude does have the power to make all your wishes come true.

If someone gave you his word that if you drank a potion from a specific vial, all your dreams would become reality, you are likely to give that person your attention and drink from the vial, right? Well, gratitude is a magical potion that can do all these things for you. By simply building an appreciative mindset, you can cultivate the life you have always desired: a beautiful life you deserve to live and enjoy.

Here is how you can cultivate this state of mind.

How to Create the Gratitude State of Mind

Creating the gratitude mindset can be as complicated or as simple as you want it to be. If you are committed to becoming a thankful, kind, and humble individual who is all set to harness the power of gratitude and who is ready to pay attention to his blessings and be thankful for them, you will easily be able to do so. However, if it takes you time to settle and adjust to your current life, focus on your blessings, and let go of things you want but do not have, nurturing gratitude and harnessing its power will take time. The choice is yours and the power to do it lies within you.

Ungratefulness and gratefulness are states of your mind you nurture consciously or unconsciously. A lack of gratitude and gratitude are intangible in nature, and solely reside in your mind. The state of mind you nurture brings similar but measurable and tangible results to different aspects of your life. In other words, every thought you nurture and consistently focus on casts a certain influence on your life.

Similarly, if you nurture an ungrateful state of mind, every probability is that you are unhappy with your life. When you consistently and incessantly think that, you strengthen your ungrateful thoughts; consequently, this brings similar experiences towards you. If you keep thinking you are poor and feel unhappy about it, you will forever stay that way. Why is this so? Because when you are unhappy with your current state in life, you will always complain about it instead of looking for ways to improve it. On top of that, you will send negative, unthankful thoughts to the universe. When you send negative thoughts out into the universe, you get negative experiences in return.

On the other hand, if you choose to be grateful, you shall start focusing on all you currently have. If you do not own a big house, at least you have a small apartment, and a roof over your head. If you do not own a car, at least you have money to spend on transportation. Similarly, you shall start acknowledging all the little gifts you have. This will help you build a grateful state of mind, which as you already know, will do wonders for you.

This shows that **everything** begins with a thought in your mind. Before you can manifest anything, you must think about it, and **how** you think about it plays a monumental role in shaping your reality. You may have unconsciously developed ungratefulness: it may have crept inside you and found an abode in your mind through different cues in your environment. To develop conscious gratefulness, you must remain consistently and consciously deliberate about it.

Since everything begins in your mind and you have complete control and choice over how to shape your life, you can consciously nurture gratitude. Small efforts consciously made will help you cultivate this beautiful state of mind, and in time, you will reap miraculous benefits.

At first, you shall not realize how amazing its power is. In the start, you will just find yourself feeling happy and mildly relaxed about everything and your life. But if you consistently keep practicing gratitude, you will bring these effects to your relationships, finances, health, profession, and every other aspect of your life.

If you are ready to make this effort, simply be more conscious of the things you have in your life. Make it a habit to look for any 3 qualities in yourself every morning and appreciate yourself for those qualities. After noticing these three things and being thankful for them, thank the universe for blessing you with such amazing strengths. This helps you become content with yourself, which in turn increases your self-esteem; allowing you to believe in yourself, and constantly perform at your peak.

Secondly, eliminate the words/ phrases such as "I do not have blessing X (name of anything you do not have)," "I cannot do this because I don't have this" and other similar phrases that show you cannot achieve your goals because you lack something.

To be thankful for your life and thus, make it better, you need to eradicate such a mentality. Consciously try doing this every time you think of something that makes you feel discontent. To replace ungratefulness with gratefulness, quickly think of any blessing you have. If you consciously do this a few times daily, you will soon nurture the habit of thinking positively and being thankful for your life. This helps you build a thankful state of mind that then helps you exploit and employ the power of gratitude.

Along with gratitude, to channelize the power of the universe towards manifesting your desires, you need forgiveness. Let us talk about it next.

Chapter 8

Forgive

"To err is human; to forgive, divine." –
Alexander Pope

Divine is the power of the Universal Mind. To harness it, you must do something divine too. This is where forgiveness comes in

To many of us, forgiveness, whether it is forgiving those close to us or ourselves, does not come easy. Letting go of the hurt someone caused you and forgiving that person after he or she has wronged you is not as simple as it sounds. How can you compel your heart to be merciful? How can you just let go of all the anger and hate, and truly forgive?

Moreover, forgiving yourself could be just as difficult. Undoubtedly, your past is full of mistakes, and the many setbacks you experience make you feel unworthy and unhappy. When you lowly regard yourself, you will not value yourself. This will cause you to be harsh on yourself whenever you err and falter. Even worse, you will not believe in yourself. You will not supply yourself with the support you need to become the impactful, powerful, and significant person you can truly be. You must learn to forgive yourself; from there, you will let go of what was, and focus on **what can be.**

Let us talk more about forgiveness so you can understand its essence and importance in your life.

Forgiveness Cleanses You of Toxic Emotions

"Because forgiveness is like this: a room can be dark because you have closed the windows, you've closed the curtains, but the sun is shining outside, and the air is fresh outside. In order to get that fresh air, you have to get up and open the window and draw apart the curtains." – **Desmond Tutu**

To bring some fresh air and light into your life, to rejuvenate yourself, to be happy, and calm—to let go of worries and negativities, to cleanse yourself of undesirable emotions, to completely believe in yourself—and to purify your beliefs of negative elements, you must become forgiving. Like gratefulness, forgiveness is a state of mind: one that can rid you completely of toxic emotions and uneasiness, and help you create a joyous, serene, and successful life.

Forgiveness is a process through which you voluntarily change your attitude, emotions, and feelings about a certain event or person, and let go of any sort of negative emotion you are harboring. If someone has hurt you and you choose to forgive that person, you decide not to avenge this hurt and instead concentrate on yourself, and move forward.

To let go of bitterness and resentment so you can manifest peace and tranquility, you must cultivate forgiveness within your life. When you hold grudges, you focus your thoughts negativity, and on taking revenge on the person who has hurt you. This clutters your mind with negative and unwanted thoughts, and keeps you from deeply focusing on your desires. To keep your mind clutter-free and to strengthen your positive beliefs, you must forgive: **others** and **yourself**.

Self-Forgiveness Strengthens Your Positive Beliefs

"Forgive yourself for your faults and your mistakes and move on." – **Les Brown**

To believe in yourself, let go of negative thoughts, explore your desires, understand your genuine needs, and to build the positivity you need to materialize them, you must accept and forgive yourself entirely: **inside**, and **out**. Accepting yourself is critical to building strong, positive beliefs. However, this does not mean you should feel happy about your shortcomings and or do nothing to improve them.

It just means you accept the fact that you are an individual who has some strengths and weaknesses, and has the potential to move on. It means you do not let your weaknesses and the mistakes of your past overpower your thinking, and you do not allow yourself to disregard your strengths. Instead, you acknowledge your personal assets, become determined to overcome your weaknesses, and start to believe in yourself - which as you already know, is essential to creating a successful and fulfilling life.

You cannot practice self-acceptance until you practice self-forgiveness because if you are not ready to make peace with your past mistakes and let them go, you will never fully accept your existence and individuality. To make your life worthwhile, you must move forward; this can only happen when you choose to forgive.

By forgiving yourself as well as others, you will release yourself from the prison of hurtful memories; Instead of feeling stuck somewhere in the past, you will have the courage to get up and move forward. If you are finding this hard to believe, try this little exercise:

Think of any regrets you have and visualize them. Build a detailed scenario where you see yourself making the mistake you regret. Next, loudly, clearly, and slowly say, "I forgive completely and whole heartedly myself for what I did and I choose to move on." Utter each word as slowly and loudly as you can and let its vibration ring in your ear.

With your eyes closed, keep uttering this sentence for 50 repeats. Open your eyes once you have said it 50 times and now observe your feelings about that experience. Your hurtful and negative feelings are likely to have dampened, and you should feel more at peace.

Now think of anything you cannot forgive someone else for and visualize that scenario. If your ex-boyfriend betrayed you, an experience that still makes you feel terrible, and you are yet to forgive him, think of that. Say 'I forgive X (name of person) for what he/she did to me. I have peace for X in my heart." Just as you did with the previous suggestion, say this 50 times too.

By the time you end the practice, you will feel much lighter and will have forgiven that person. Practice this exercise daily for a few minutes; it will help you let go of any hurtful memory, and completely forgive whoever it is you must.

By forgiving yourself and all those who have hurt you, you allow yourself to stop living in the past and start dwelling in the present. This allows your thoughts of the present to flow freely, and aid you in acknowledging them.

When you acknowledge your present, you cultivate immense gratitude and start to believe in yourself. This means every positive and negative emotion has a connection. To reap the benefits of one emotion, you must nurture the one connected to it.

To become grateful, you need to be forgiving and when you have gratitude, you automatically start forgiving others just as much as you forgive yourself. Forgiveness and gratitude go hand in hand indeed. To live in the present and make the best use of it, you must let go of your past; forgiveness helps you do that.

Here is how you can practice forgiveness to build that state of mind.

How to Nurture the Habit of Being Forgiving

Forgiveness is both easy and difficult to develop. Easy if you make conscious efforts to be forgiving and understand that forgiveness, like other emotions, begins with your thoughts; difficult if you stay stubborn and fail to make any conscious effort to melt your strong, negative thoughts of hate or resentment.

If you are ready to make a conscious effort to make forgiveness a part of your life, try the following tactics.

Let Go of Your Mistakes and Failures: If you have made mistakes in the past or gone through failures you are not proud of, jot them down in your journal and visualize that scenario. Now chant a forgiveness based affirmation such as "I forgive myself for my mistakes and choose to move forward" a few times.

Next, think of any positive point or lesson you learned from that experience; this will help turn that memory into a positive one. If you feel bad that you ended your 4 year-long marriage, focus on why you did that. Perhaps you divorced your spouse because he did not treat you nicely and because of the divorce, you now lead a happier life.

Similarly, look for any good brought about by any bad situation; this will help you feel more positive about it, and you will quickly forgive yourself for it. Practice this exercise each time you make a mistake in the present too.

Accept Your Individuality: Secondly, be more understanding and appreciative of your individuality. If you feel different and separate from the rest of the world, have a different sexual orientation than the world expects of you, or have any other special/different element that makes you stand out, acknowledge, and appreciate that.

You were born to be different and extraordinary and for you to fully accept yourself, you must feel proud of who you truly are. Just make sure your individuality and your genuine needs/desires match; if they do, you have no reason to hide or be ashamed of **anything**.

Be Kind with Yourself: Thirdly, start talking more kindly and politely to yourself. Whenever you make a mistake or experience difficulty executing a task as you planned, do not criticize yourself. Instead, be polite with yourself and forgive yourself. Tell yourself to make a fresh start and give yourself lots of flexibility and time. This helps you treat every day as a new start, and make the most of them.

Along with this, this will powerfully strengthen your self-belief; forgive yourself for your mistakes, tell yourself that you **can** and **will** improve, and then **act**.

Stop Hating People: To forgive all those who have hurt you so you can stop nurturing hateful feelings for them, practice the forgiveness-based affirmation stated earlier.

People wrong each other all the time and therefore, if someone has wronged you, you have probably done something bad to somebody else too. If you cannot bring yourself to forgive someone, you have no one but yourself to blame for not receiving forgiveness from the person you have hurt too. Let go of that hate and be courageous enough to forgive.

Think of the situation and put yourself in the other person's shoes. If you were in the person's situation at that time, perhaps you would have done the same, something similar, or something worse. See that memory from this perspective and you will find your stance towards forgiving that person softening.

Take Responsibility for Your Mistakes: Moreover, start taking responsibility for your mistakes. Sometimes we feel that others are the cause of certain situations in our lives and we blame them for the mess we are currently dealing with. What we forget is that we are the ones who gave those people that authority in the first place and if we trusted the wrong people, the wrongdoing is on our shoulders, not theirs.

For instance, if you allowed your brother to make decisions for you, which is why you chose a wrong job/profession, that mistake is yours; quit blaming your brother for your miserable career life. You gave your brother the authority to decide for you and as such, you are responsible for making the wrong decision in the first place.

Similarly, there will be many such instances where you blame others for your problems. Quit doing so and instead, analyze all those instances, man up, and take responsibility for your mistakes. Stop playing the blame game and become accountable for your life. The moment you adopt this approach, you feel less resentful of others and more determined about bringing a positive change in your life.

Set Boundaries: Lastly, start setting healthy boundaries for yourself and for everyone else in your life. A lack of boundaries is precisely what allows others to take advantage of you, meddle in your life, and then hurt you.

Continuing with the earlier example, you never set any boundary for your brother, which is why he did not know when to stop making decisions for you or consider your wishes. Had you set limits for him, you would not have given him the authority to interfere with your personal decisions.

Start setting healthy boundaries for all the people in your life and communicate those boundaries to them. Let them know how much authority, say, and interference they can have in your life, and to what extent you can pay heed to them. In addition, start saying no to people who misuse your kindness, those who make you run countless errands for them. Such people are misusing your energy and keeping you from utilizing your own power.

Set boundaries for yourself so you know to what extent you can help others and focus on the; this will help you start making more time for yourself. Naturally, when you pay attention to your needs and desires, you focus more on manifesting them, which helps you move on and live a good life.

Work on these guidelines so you can become more forgiving and successful in life. Lastly, to create a meaningful life, you need to be selfishly selfless. Since this is contrary to most of what we have thus far discussed in this book, you may feel a bit confused. The next chapter clears all your ambiguities.

Chapter 9

Be Selfish to Be Selfless

"Your conscience is the measure of the honesty of your selfishness. Listen to it carefully." – **Richard Bach**

All of us have different potentials, and different purposes and goals in life. None of us are the same as another. Because we are different, we have different dreams and different aspirations and want to live our life a certain way. For that to happen, being selfishly selfless is crucial.

What Does Being Selfishly Selfless Mean?

Being selfishly selfless means first focusing on your needs and desires so you can know your talents, gifts, and potentials, polish them, and then selflessly use them to improve the world and your immediate society. Unless you are selfish at first, you will never get the time, energy, and strength to focus on yourself; you will forever bow down to the wishes and needs of others.

If you look around you, you will see many loved ones. Your loved ones are your teachers, siblings, friends, family, and other people who care about you. These people love you and if they are sincere with you, they have your best interests at heart.

Nevertheless, even when they have your interest at heart, they want you to do things for them, behave a certain way, and be a certain type of person. For instance, your father may love you a lot but he may want you to join the army instead of starting business. Your wife cares deeply for you and she may want you to help her with her business instead of pursuing your own. Similarly, every person around you expects you to do something.

Your loved ones want you to be amazing and they are trying to help you get there, but what these people fail to understand is that you are a different individual with personal needs, demands, and desires. You have lived life differently and they cannot see everything through your eyes. By being submissive to them, you allow them to control you and when you do this, you let go of your genuine desires and the power to manifest them.

To prove your worth to this world, to live life as you want, and to feel free and amazing, you need a degree of selfishness. Until you dare be selfish, you will not manifest your desires.

In the beginning, you need to be selfish enough to focus on your needs, know your desires, and work strenuously to develop and polish your skills. Only after developing the ability to fulfill your desires can you use your power to help everyone around you in your own unique way.

For instance, if you desire to be surfer but your parents want you to be a doctor, listen to and follow your heart. Perhaps they want you to be a doctor so that later in life, you can earn a good living and support them. You can do the same if you become a great surfer. By being a surfer, you can help others realize their passion for surfing and teach them the art of surfing.

Everyone in this world is a gifted individual: all of us have unique powers, but many of us are unaware of them simply because we are not selfish enough to dig deeper into ourselves and discover our potential. We settle for what we receive while deep down, we feel sad about it. To stop feeling that way, start being selfish. Doing so will be tough but its results will be amazing for sure.

Once you fulfill your desires and have skills you can use to help others, you can help others around you realize their potential and genuine desires and then help them actualize them. Once you know the drill, guiding others will be easy and you shall be in a position to help others manifest a good life for themselves too.

How to be Selfishly Selfless

Here is what you need to do to be selfish to become selfless.

- First, weed out all the naysayers in your life who keep pulling you down and barraging you with negativity. All the people who tell you it is not possible to live your dreams, all those who feed negative ideas to your brain, and all those who make you feel bad about yourself fall in this category. Slowly distance yourself from these people so you can keep yourself safe from the harms of their polluting thoughts.

- Secondly, spend time with positive people who encourage you to believe in yourself and who, courtesy of their strong, positive beliefs, have created a good life for themselves. Such people will influence you to be better.

- Thirdly, make time for your needs. Find out what you yearn for, are destined to do, and create action plans that help you manifest those desires. If you are sure about achieving a certain goal but someone in your life tells you otherwise, do not listen to that person, such a person does not know you or your wants: you are the boss of your life and therefore, you call all the shots.

- Make sure you always stay focused on your desires and keep feeding positive, yourself inspirational mental food by listening to good and inspirational lectures, reading good books, and watching influential movies/documentaries.

- Say no to all those who bombard you with their wishes and demands and let them know that your focus is on your work first. At first, rejecting people and their wishes is hard, but doing so is the only way to focus on yourself. Once you have manifested your goals, you can work for others too. If you do not concentrate on your desires now, you will forever remain stuck in your life and will never feel good about yourself. A journey of a thousand miles starts with a single step. You have to take that step right now by being selfish.

Being selfish is not bad at all. In fact, it is healthy to focus on your needs and stand for your rights. Being selfish is the only way you better yourself to a point where later, you can do good things for others.

Remember that being self-less does not mean you have to give away your stuff to others or give up everything you own. If giving away your things is what brings you happiness, you can do that. However, the main point to being selfless is selflessly working for the good of society: to help others become better. You can do this only after you have bettered yourself, which calls for a level of selfishness.

Conclusion

We have come to the end of the book. Thank you for reading and congratulations for reading until the end.

I truly hope that you have gathered valuable information in the book and are excited to start taking action after setting an intention to change your negative beliefs to positive ones.

"Imagine with all your mind, believe with all your heart, and achieve with all your might." – **Unknown**

Believing in yourself and your power, and visualizing what you want to achieve are indeed keys to success. This book has provided you sufficient knowledge and actionable information on how to achieve success by creating a mindset favorable to it. Now the ball is in your court.

Implement the information in this book, and become the proud creator of an amazing reality.

Always remember; reading this book and taking action is the first step. The change in belief system might not take place overnight. But if you are consistent at it, you can be sure that you will see massive transformations in your life. And as Jim Rohn put it; *"you cannot change your destination overnight, but you can change your direction overnight."* I believe this book has helped you change the direction your life has been taking for years towards your dream destination. Just keep at it and soon, you will get there.

If you found the book valuable, can you recommend it to others? One way to do that is to post a review on Amazon.

Made in the USA
Columbia, SC
01 September 2017